W9-CMT-380

THE
PERFECT
CUP

A
COFFEE-LOVER'S
GUIDE
TO
BUYING,
BREWING,
and
TASTING

TIMOTHY JAMES CASTLE

Aris Books

Addison-Wesley Publishing Company
Reading, Massachusetts   Menlo Park, California   New York
Don Mills, Ontario   Wokingham, England   Amsterdam   Bonn
Sydney   Singapore   Tokyo   Madrid   San Juan   Paris
Seoul   Milan   Mexico City   Taipei

The recipe "Russian Black Bread" originally appeared in *Bernard Clayton's New Complete Book of Breads* by Brenard Clayton. Copyright © 1987 by Bernard Clayton. Reprinted by permission of Simon & Schuster, Inc.

The recipe "Carne de Res con Café" originally appeared in *False Tongues and Sunday Bread* by Copeland Marks. Copyright © 1985 by Copeland Marks. Reprinted with permission from M. Evans and Company, Inc.

The recipe "Tiramisu," copyright © 1989 by Chianti Ristorante, is reprinted with permission from Spectrum Foods, Inc.

The recipe "Valentino," copyright © 1990 by Ciao, is reprinted with permission from Spectrum Foods, Inc.

Swiss Water and logo are trademarks licensed to Swiss Water Decaf Divison, Nabob Foods, Ltd.

Many of the designations used by manufacturers and sellers to distinguish their products are claimed as trademarks. Where those designations appear in this book and Addison-Wesley was aware of a trademark claim, the designations have been printed in initial capital letters (e.g., Kahlúa).

Library of Congress Cataloging-in-Publication Data

Castle, Timothy James.
  The Perfect cup : a coffee lover's guide to buying, brewing, and tasting / Timothy James Castle.
    p.   cm.
  Includes index.
  ISBN 0-201-53850-4 (paper)
  1. Coffee.   I.   Title.
  TX817.c6c37   1991
  641.6´ 373—dc20   90-45505
                                                     CIP

Copyright © 1991 by Timothy James Castle

All rights reserved. No part of this publication may be reproduced, stored in a retrieval system, or transmitted, in any from or by any means, electronic, mechanical, photocopying, recording, or otherwise, without the prior written permission of the publisher. Printed in the United States of America. Published simultaneously in Canada.

Text design by Ruth Kolbert
Illustrated by Bob Giuliani
Jacket photograph © by Simon Metz
Jacket design by Diana Coe
Set in 11-point Bembo by G&S Typesetters, Austin, TX

A B C D E -ALG-96 95 94 93 92

ACKNOWLEDGMENTS

Being in the business of selling coffee and simultaneously trying to write about it has been an interesting experience. My customers deserve much of the credit for this book's coming into being. I would like to thank them first for the business, knowledge, and friendship they have extended to me over the years. My suppliers, also, deserve much credit for the good information this book has to offer and the fact that it is here at all. I hope both groups will forgive me for avoiding the obvious perils of listing one and all.

There are actually very few people in the coffee industry whom I would *not* thank. The coffee trade (both specialty and commercial) is one of the best groups of people I've ever encountered, and I am honored to play a small part in it. I extend a genuine, heartfelt thank you to the industry, without reservation.

This book would not have been possible without the contributions of the people I work with at Castle & Company and Castle Communications: Chris Perri and

Mark Woods, the men who "move the coffee" in our office—two solid guys with whom I am very proud to be working; Betty Nowling, whose constant attention to detail, whose focus and commitment have saved the day on many occasions; Haimanodt Habtu, whose pleasant disposition and steady performance are much appreciated; Greg Pittler, with whom I've worked for five years, and will I hope, for many years to come; Melissa Pugash, whose hard work, long hours, and dedication helped transform a hobby into the real business called Castle Communications; and Joan Hackeling, who has become a fine writer and designer over the years and who is ceaselessly professional.

There are others, closer to this book, to whom I also owe a debt of gratitude:

I would like to acknowledge the help and support of Irene S. Phelps, with whom I share my life. Thank you, Irene.

John Harris, of Aris/Addison-Wesley, whose patience prevented the demise of this book. His help in guiding this book in its development was an essential contribution.

Martha Casselman, my agent, whose patience was tested only somewhat less than her memory by the slow evolution of this book.

Wendy Rasmussen Moore helped to write this book. The interviews with roaster-retailers and farmer-growers are hers. The rest of the book was written by me and was thoroughly edited by Ms. Moore. This book would still be a hypothetical enterprise were it not for her.

A special thank you to George Howell of Coffee Connection in Boston, who made himself and his store available for the purpose of illustrating this book.

Finally, my parents, Diane and Alex, who made it possible for me to get started in the coffee business, and shared with me their enthusiasm for flavors and tastes.

CONTENTS

FOREWORD

I FIRST MET TIM CASTLE WHEN I WAS IN SEARCH OF a Virgil who would introduce me to the mysterious world of coffee. I was embarking on a series of articles on the subject for *The Atlantic* and had everything to learn. No one better to teach me, it turned out, than a young man whose expertise and enthusiasm were already much vaunted. On two coasts I heard that Castle was one of the few people able to put frustratingly technical information into easily comprehensible terms, someone who studied the rewarding balances of food and wine and knew how to extend them to coffee.

Without hesitation, Castle brought me to places I wouldn't have known to ask to go—a small coffee roaster, for example, who let me watch and sniff while he took a batch of green beans and made them a beautiful, gleaming brown, and then a larger high-quality roasting company where I learned about the newest packaging to keep beans at their freshest and was moved by the tremendous pride of one family dedicated for generations to making their customers' coffee taste good.

Finally, Castle led me to a fabled cupping—the serious and methodical sampling of scores of little cups of coffee, which usually takes place in a back room at a round table surrounded by gruff men in shirtsleeves. In one chapter here Castle entertainingly describes the cupping ritual, but he modestly doesn't describe his own regular transformation into a member of the small, international tribe of coffee buyers, a tribe of laconic and extremely knowledgeable men who "never let on that they have memories like encyclopedias and minds like calculators," as he once told me.

Now Castle will show you what those men look for but rarely talk about, in a book unlike any I have read on coffee. It straddles the line between the beginner who has never thought to go beyond the deli coffee at the corner and the coffee-lover who would like to become a connoisseur. It teaches you to learn to taste for yourself, and bravely takes on the challenge of defining a taste vocabulary, something that doesn't exist for coffee. Castle sorts through the many catch phrases used in the coffee business and distills them so that they make sense—a task that is much harder than it sounds, and one that has tripped up many worthy writers.

He also gives a brief atlas of coffee that will help you associate more useful information with exotic places like Java and Malabar and Santos than something you might have read in a guide book. Castle debunks the myths that have grown up around Jamaican and Kona coffee, urging instead an appreciation for the subtler world of the many other wonderful coffees that high-quality shops regularly stock.

Where to find those wonderful coffees? Castle takes the reader across the United States to describe the enormous range of styles of coffee made by different roasters devoted to the bean. He gives shrewd, affectionate delineations of some of the principal characters in the coffee business today, adding entertaining vignettes of, say, very busy roasters at the end of the day emptying green beans out of their socks. One man speaks for his customers when he says, "No matter what kind of a day they're having, they smell the coffee and they smile." Many of these independent merchants don't agree with each other in the least (or with Castle, for that matter), but each thinks that his way guarantees the best-tasting coffee. That leaves you poised to make your own coffee expedition.

Castle champions the people who grow coffee and how the attention they pay to nurturing it can make a difference in the cup. He has visited many coffee plantations, and he is passionate about connecting the sun, wind, rain, and earth to the final savor of a cup of coffee. "Some coffees bring with them the smells of the forests they grew near," he writes, "the taste of the water that soaked their roots, the flavors of the fruits that grew near them. And if a cup of coffee simply tastes good, it's not as great as the one that reminds you it came from a *place* and that *people* grew it; in fact they worked hard enough that your coffee reminds you that sun-gnarled hands pulled each cherry from the tree." Few words could be more essential to a real understanding of coffee.

In his travels as coffee trader and ambassador, Castle often carries little bags of extraordinary coffee to offer to people he encounters outside the coffee business. The rare delicacy of his seemingly small gift is often lost on its recipient. Like Johnny Appleseed, but with another kind of seed, Castle is scattering coffee beans on whatever ground he can find, trying to sow appreciation for the variety and depth of fine coffees. "Good coffee can become clear," Castle maintains, "to anyone willing to take the time and energy to discover it." This book shows you how.

CORBY KUMMER

INTRODUCTION

THERE'S A NEW BEVERAGE IN AMERICA. IT'S BLACK, with a deep amber glow and an intoxicating aroma. Its cousin, a brew with a greenish complexion and sour disposition, has enjoyed a long reign on supermarket shelves and TV screens across America. Both the emerging beverage and its ubiquitous relative are known by the name *coffee*. This is a book about the beverage America is falling in love with: "gourmet coffee" to some, "specialty coffee" to others, and "whole-bean coffee" to those who insist on the most objective definition.

There is a real distinction between specialty or gourmet coffee and the "Java" Americans have been drinking for decades, and it's based primarily on the fact that there are two commercially popular species of coffee, one called *Coffea arabica,* and the other *Coffea robusta.* The **arabica** coffee tree produces the higher-quality beans. **Robusta** beans are the main component in canned ground coffee (see also pages 11 through 15).

The beans for the better decoction, although increasingly available, are still sold primarily in small stores, where they are labeled by their country of origin, degree of roast, or as proprietary blends, often with romantic names and jealously guarded proportions. For the purposes of this book, I will refer to coffees from the **arabica** species as specialty coffee. One could just as easily call these *gourmet* coffees, but in the coffee market this is an overused word with tired implications, like the word *natural* in the health foods industry.

While it is well known to the devoted coffeeholic, specialty coffee represents less than 8 percent of all the coffee consumed in America. Specialty coffee consumption has been increasing steadily for the past fifteen years, while overall per capita consumption has decreased or remained the same every year from 1961 to 1990. In response to this trend major roasters have begun to upgrade their coffees (and intensify their advertising) in an effort to recapture the quality-conscious consumer. It appears to be working, as coffee consumption has shown signs of leveling off rather than decreasing since 1985.

All across America, coffee-making equipment is available in dizzying variety in department stores, boutique coffee shops, and specialty kitchen stores. Twenty years ago only the library could provide information on the subject of specialty coffee, and the names of the great coffee estates, the roasting houses, and the roastmasters were faint memories. (As a child my grandfather remembers walking down to the local A&P with the few necessary quarters to buy half a pound of Mocha and half a pound of Java for his mother's morning cup: whole beans, freshly roasted. This was before coffee became a mega-business and the technology of cheapening it was fully perfected.) Today the local yellow pages in any sizable American town will lead the way to several retailers who can not only provide some of the best coffee available but who, along with their distributors and brokers, can provide detailed responses to even the most arcane inquiries regarding coffee.

While still a minor economic phenomenon, the increasing popularity of specialty coffees reflects a growing concern and desire for quality in food and beverage (and general lifestyle). We are no longer content with "generic" potatoes, rice, wheat, beef, fish, vegetables, and dairy products, but are seeking foods that reflect conscientious decisions regarding flavor, texture, and aroma on the part of those who produce for us.

As our interest in the sources of our foods increases, so too does our interest in the methods of production and the people who implement those methods. In the world of coffee, this phenomenon is reflected by the fact that coffee growers around the world are paying attention to increased consumer demand for quality and style. In the chapter on coffee farming, you will find first-hand accounts of coffee growers, processors, and shippers from various coffee-producing areas of the world. A few years ago many of these producers lamented the deteriorating condition of the quality market and the farms that supplied it, but their story today is a happier one.

The American romance with specialty coffee is still fresh, but also somewhat restrained. Purists will argue that the perfect cup should be brewed simply and drunk hot and black. Yet ever since its discovery, coffee has been used as a flavoring agent in other drinks, in desserts, and even in meat and fowl dishes. It's time to expand awareness of the uses of coffee, and so this book includes recipes that use coffee as a flavoring and some general tips on cooking with coffee.

As I look back over the five years of writing this book, I marvel at my presumptuousness at beginning a comprehensive book on coffee after seven years' experience in the business. This material includes, either directly through interviews or indirectly through questions asked and experiences shared, the contributions of the many people

whom I've had the pleasure of sharing the exciting new industry of specialty coffee with. The sum total has much to do with the energy and determination of my customers, suppliers, and competitors.

I hope the reader is able to gain from this book more appreciation for a good cup of coffee, not only in terms of flavor, taste, and aroma but in the awareness of the amount of human involvement that the "perfect" cup of coffee requires. A pound of coffee contains roughly two thousand beans, each of which had to be hand picked and in many cases hand sorted. A good strong cup of coffee requires a brewing ratio of one pound for every forty cups, meaning that each cup contains the extraction of fifty hand-picked beans. Every step of coffee production requires the same kind of concern, effort, and consideration. Most specialty coffees sell for under ten dollars, but even with an expensive estate coffee at twelve dollars a pound, you can experience one of the world's most carefully cultivated handmade products for thirty cents a cup.

Introduction

Most luxuries in life are reserved for the few who can afford the expense that they command, but a great cup of coffee is relatively low in cost and provides employment for countless millions of people throughout the world. While the production of lower-quality coffee often involves harsh working conditions, the growing of good coffee provides a higher quality of life for everyone involved. Providing the information necessary to gain access to the enjoyment of better coffee is the goal of this book.

Given that it would probably be impossible for someone in the coffee business to write an "objective" coffee book, I didn't even try. The opinions expressed in this book are, taken as a whole, a case of personal preference run rampant. Cynics will say that preference has been derived from commercial interest: let them. I believe, in any event, that it is in my commercial interest for the reader to find his or her way to a better cup of coffee, and I am convinced that this book can help.

Specifically, the reader should know that I currently have marketing arrangements with La Minita Terazú, San Sebastian Antigua, and other coffees herein mentioned. Also, we have sold a lot of KVW process decaffeinated and are currently negotiating to do business with Swiss Water processors. In fact, if there is any coffee mentioned in an extremely favorable light, the reader should assume that I either offer it for sale, or would like to very badly.

As for the selection of roasters interviewed, similar conflicts of interest prevail. I would like to modify that only slightly by saying that some of the roasters mentioned have never bought a bean from me.

All of this is to remind the reader that when it comes to aesthetic judgments, there is no greater truth than one's own experience. And your own experience is the only path to your perfect cup.

GETTING
TO KNOW
BEANS
about
COFFEE

COFFEE ISN'T A FLAVOR BUT A COMPLEX OF FLA-
vors, tastes, and aromas. You, your memories, and your unconscious will latch onto one set of
aromatics and ignore others, making coffee a very particular experience. Strawberries, pineapples, and hazelnuts all
have one chemical compound that will singularly denote
their source, but with coffee the experience is more personal and ephemeral. If you don't finish your cup while it's
at its short-lived peak, you might as well forget what's left.
Coffee isn't a liquid so much as a chemical reaction in
progress, and the soul of the brew will twist out of the cup
in an instant if not attended to.

But what about the coffee drinker who uses canned
ground coffee from the local supermarket? The coffee experience just described may seem far from the comforting
morning aroma and jolt of caffeine he is used to. For him,
taste may be a secondary consideration for obtaining the
desired physiological effects.

And then there are those, somewhere between the extremes, who know that coffee offers more than a morning or afternoon pick-me-up, that there is pleasure and subtlety in coffee, but who are only beginning to gain the experience and tools to appreciate it.

To provide a link between the experiences of all coffee drinkers, from the connoisseur to the simple consumer, we need a common language. Learning this language won't require a passport or a stay at the Berlitz Institute. The tools to discovering specialty coffee are the taste buds, the imagination, and a willingness to remember and to attach words to sensory images.

• A Word About the Plant •

Coffee belongs to the family Rubiacaeae, genus *Coffea*, which originated in the tropic parts of Africa, Ethiopia, and Yemen, and then with the help of human intervention spread to other continents. Of the numerous different species of *Coffea* most are of little interest to the roaster, retailer, or consumer. *Coffea* is botanically divided into four groups, the only one of importance to us being *eucoffea*. Of the other three groups, some are used as decorative vegetation and some are utilized by the native culture for stimulant value, but their fruit is often inedible and they have no economic viability. *Eucoffea* covers the following groups: *erythrocoffea, nanocoffea, pachycoffea, melanocoffea,* and *mozambicoffea*. A listing of these groups and the important species they cover can be found in more technical sources such as Bernard Rothfos's *Coffee Production* (Gordian-Max-Rieck Gmbh Hamburg, 1980).

Worth special mention, however, is the plant *Coffea stenophylla*. According to Paul Leighton of the Coffee Corner in Eugene, Oregon, *stenophylla* by historical accounts was considered to be better than **arabica,** the most important coffee species for making fine coffee; the plant is hardier, it produces more, and the final commodity has a better flavor. So why aren't we finding it in our cups? The answer lies in timing. The plant was discovered in West Africa and introduced to various English colonies in 1895–96. At this time in coffee-producing history, however, there were tremendous problems with rust disease, and many plantations were wiped out. To recoup their losses farms needed a plant that would produce as quickly as possible. *Stenophylla* takes a total of nine years, two years longer than **arabica,** to reach maturity, even though it's hardier and produces more after reaching the producing stage. In the quest for immediate financial gratification, *stenophylla* has fallen entirely out of favor. So for our purposes, there are only two species of coffee of commercial importance, *Coffea arabica* and *Coffea canephora* (known in the trade as **robusta**). *Coffea arabica* is the species of tree from which the higher-quality specialty coffees come. **Robusta** is used as a source of cheap blenders and also as the basis of instant coffees.

Referred to in botanical references as a shrub, the coffee plant can grow to a height of ten meters, but is generally kept trimmed to three meters on coffee plantations to facilitate harvesting methods and to maintain the tree's optimum shape. The coffee plant is classified as a perennial evergreen dicotyledon, which means it is a plant that is always green and has two seeds per fruit body (in this case, a cherry). At three to four years of age the tree produces its first flowers, which are creamy white and sweet smelling. These flowers fade and give rise to oval berries that are first green, and then ripen to a bright red. At this point they are commonly referred to as cherries, and are harvested for processing into green coffee. Like most things in life, none of this happens at the same time. It is not uncommon to find flowers, green berries, and ripe cherries all on the same branch, especially in areas that have consistent rainfall throughout the year. The problems this creates are discussed in the section on harvesting (see page 167).

The coffee beans that reach your roaster are the seeds from the ripe cherries, devoid of the fleshy pulp and processed according to the method of that country or estate. Each seed, or bean, is covered with a thin, close-fitting tegument called the silverskin, outside of which is a looser, yellowish skin called the parchment. Coffee may be delivered in its green state with the silverskin attached, and, although not common, parchment-covered samples may also be sent. During the development of the seeds inside the cherry, one of the two may fail to develop. This causes the remaining seed to form a round cross-section, known in the trade as a "peaberry." There is a belief in the trade that peaberries, due to their unique development, result in more flavorful coffees, but I have never been able to detect a consistent difference.

The plant we are concerned with, *C. arabica,* constitutes 80 percent of the world's coffee production. A native of Ethiopia, it continues to grow wild in the high mountains where it originated. Since its discovery by Middle Eastern countries in the fifteenth century, however, its cultivation has spread throughout the world. Today, coffee is a major crop in fifty-two countries throughout Africa, the Americas, Asia, and Oceania. There are a number of forms of **arabica,** the result both of purposeful breeding and of spontaneous mutations in the field. Of these various forms, two are considered the "original" varieties: *C. arabica arabica* (or *typica*), and *C. arabica bourbon.* Of the other forms, *C. arabica Maragogype* is one you might occasionally encounter. Resulting from a mutation on a Brazilian plantation in 1870, this can be described as a gigantic version of *C. arabica,* for the leaves, fruit, and seeds of this plant are all larger. During the Second World War, this variety was widely planted to produce caffeine for soldiers and fighter pilots. Despite the less-than-spectacular end product, "marigo" beans later enjoyed a short-lived popularity in Germany where bean "style" was a strong consideration, as the marigo beans, being twice the size of regular coffee beans, have an attractive appearance when roasted.

Currently, there are many varieties of *Coffea arabica* in commercial production. *Cattura* and *catuai* are two hybrids that grow much shorter than *bourbon* and *typica* and are therefore much easier to harvest. In addition they are more productive and more resistant to disease than the older varieties. As the visits from specialty roasters to coffee farms become more frequent, the question arises as to whether *bourbon* and *typica* trees don't produce better-tasting coffee than the more recent hybrids. Farmers deny there is any difference at all, and specialty roasters are convinced that the farmers are trying to bar them from untold firmaments of coffee quality and knowledge. In the cup, the difference is perceptible but not dramatic. Elevation, tree husbandry,

The Original Coffee Tree

Almost all of the billions of coffee trees in Latin America derive from the same source, a heavily guarded coffee plant in the hothouse of Louis XIV's Jardin des Plantes. While other coffee plants had already made it to the New World, the most influential was a descendant of this particular plant. The story of this seedling is colored by a history of romance and intrigue. It was brought to Martinique by Capt. Gabriel de Clieu, who gained possession of it through a successful liaison with a lady of quality, who had access to the garden through the court physician. De Clieu, a young French naval officer, was supposedly inspired by patriotic zeal, for by bringing coffee to Martinique, he allowed France to become independent from high-priced East Indian coffee. The plant thrived in its new home, and its descendants are the source of most of the world's coffee today.

and processing seem to count for more. Given a choice, though, I'll take the somewhat more elegant, complex, and smooth taste of the older varieties.

The other important commercial species, *C. canephora* (from now on simply referred to as **robusta**) was not discovered growing wild until the late nineteenth century (in a landscape quite similar to that where **arabica** was originally found growing wild) near Lake Victoria in Uganda. Like the **arabica,** there are other forms of this variety, but our concern lies in the differences between **robusta** and **arabica.**

• *Robusta vs. Arabica* •

The main differences between these two commercial species are as follows: **robusta** coffee will grow at relatively low altitudes, will tolerate higher temperatures and heavier rainfall, demands higher soil humus content, and generally is more resistant to disease. **Arabica** beans tend to be oval in shape and green to pale green in color, while **robustas** are rounder and may tend towards brownish shades, and there is this essential difference: **arabicas** represent the higher-quality estate coffees found at your roaster/retailer, while **robustas** tend to be confined to the can on your grocery store shelf.

• *A Word About the Word* •

Never a wallflower, it's not likely that coffee sat around cafes, shuffled through the streets of Mecca, and prayed in mosques for a few centuries before some reflective scholar walked up and said, "Haven't I seen you here before?"

There are sweet myths and legends about coffee, beautifully recounted in other coffee books. The fact is that coffee (the beverage derived from roasted coffee beans) was first drunk in the mid-fifteenth century. Much of the confusion about its history comes from a poor understanding of a few Arabic words. First of all there's Kaffa, now more frequently spelled Kefa, a region in Ethiopia from which coffees called Djimmas (named after a city in Kefa) come. Phonetically speaking, *Kaffa* makes a lot of sense to people seeking coffee's etymological roots, but it has never been spelled *kaffa* in Arabic references, although it still appears as such in many historical accounts on coffee. For further discussion, see *Coffee and Coffeehouses* by Ralph S. Hattox (University of Washington Press).

Next, there's *qahwa,* which means (sort of), "to make undesirable," or "to lessen one's desire for something."

Qahwa, before Mohammed, usually referred to wine; it put one off food, for example.

It is important to note that we are talking about wine in the context of Arabic society (and not its upper strata either) when thinking of the name *qahwa*. Certainly at the time Mohammed banned alcohol the secular concerns surrounding the beverage were not that citizens were wasting time at vertical tastings of shiraz vintages circa the 750s A.D. The wine that "put one off" food was probably a murky and toxic fermentation of honey and fruit juice drunk to the point where food that had been consumed often ended up thoroughly unconsumed all over the drinker himself.

After Mohammed *qahwa* meant a stimulating (lessening the desire for sleep) drink made by infusing the leaves of the qat bush. It is the mention of this tea that has probably confused many writers into thinking that coffee came along much earlier than it did. Coffee also first emerged as a tea. Gradually the infusion made from the leaves of the coffee plant gave way to one made from the cherries, and finally, in the mid-1400s, sources refer to a drink made from the roasted seeds of the coffee cherry, still called *qahwa*. Many coffee scholars have also confused *quwwa* (a derivation of "power," or "strength") with *qahwa;* probably because they couldn't believe that such an ambivalent term would be used for coffee, or that the same word would have been used for wine (before it was banned by Mohammed around A.D. 622). Most books on coffee continue to propagate the notion that the word probably came from *quwwa,* while they spell out the word *qahwah*. As to the ambivalence that wine might engender we have only to turn to Shakespeare:

> . . . it provokes and it unprovokes; it provokes the desire,
> but it takes away the performance: therefore much drink
> may be said to be an equivocator with lechery: it makes him
> and it mars him; it sets him on and it takes him off; it per-

suades him and disheartens him; makes him stand to and not stand to; in conclusion, equivocates him in a sleep, and giving him the lie, leaves him. — *Macbeth,* Act II, Scene 3

While no one would ever accuse coffee of such dastardly effects, it might be conjectured that the people of Ethiopia and Yemen understood that the often-welcome stimulating effects of coffee could exact a toll later on. In any event, the word for *power,* as it is spelled in the Arabic, was never used in reference to coffee, except by scholars writing in other languages.

• *Of Historical Note* •

There is no reason to think that coffee, as we know it, was invented by any particular person or that any single chain of events led to its appearance, as many accounts would have us believe. Even the most seemingly intelligent history of coffee to date has not mentioned the possibility that a woman may have been the first to stumble across it, although women historically have been responsible for cooking, brewing, stewing, and fermenting almost everything. These seem to be more likely activities to give rise to coffee than such historical male activities as praying, writing, reading, and other preoccupations, many of which were pursued in coffeehouses after the beverage was developed.

The connoisseurship of coffee is even more recent than coffee itself. Coffee's earliest drinkers were concerned with stimulation much more than with gastronomic appreciation. Consumption in Europe and England was with the addition of generous quantities of cream and sugar. Throughout the Near and Middle East coffee was heavily sweetened and often spiced with cardamom. Considering how easy it is to produce a bad cup of coffee, and in view of some of the old recipes that recommend boiling the grounds for a half hour or more, it isn't difficult to imagine that the flavor of coffee may have been something the drinker didn't want to dwell on.

Some curious remnants of knowledge indicate a possible connoisseurship of coffee a century or more ago in Europe. Farmers of European stock remember, or heard stories from their parents, of days when the coffee industry as a whole demanded that coffee taste good in addition to being the right price. In Europe these days coffee does consistently taste somewhat better than American coffee but is not pursued with the same passion, connoisseurship, and constant inquiry into what is the best that a particular coffee or coffee-growing region can offer. The level of concern for the quality of the taste and flavor of coffee has never been greater than it is today in the U.S. specialty trade. While one hundred years ago there may have been more knowledge about how to grow better coffee, I believe that the current level of interest and curiosity will inspire a new sophistication on the part of farmers, processors, exporters, importers, and roasters that will outstrip any previously attained levels.

Why has coffee quality suffered so greatly over the past century? One answer might be that the United States population wasn't big enough to support small local roasters. The practice of roasting coffee at home, often by primitive and less than precise methods, produced inconsistent and often disastrous results, making the products of large commercial roasters enticing. And while there wasn't a lot of margin in selling the green beans, there was in selling the ground roasted product. Finally, vacuum processing made it possible for a roaster on the East Coast to sell to a grocery store in Arizona. Coffee, like a lot of other food products, suffered greatly when America fell in love with the over-application of technology.

HOW TO COMPARE
COFFEE TASTES

Cupping, or cup-testing, was developed as a means of consistently and impartially evaluating a coffee. The process, while it involves several distinct steps, is simple, especially if you take the time to acquaint yourself with the vocabulary required to describe the flavor and aromatic sensations of coffee (see page 25). This does not imply that basic vocabulary will make you a professional "cupper," which requires a tremendous investment in time and the extensive knowledge of all stages of coffee production and processing. But learning how to cup coffee will enable you

Cupping

to develop your own repertoire of great coffees, and to find the best coffee for your dollar. It is also necessary in order to discover the major characteristics of certain regions or plantations, so you can create and analyze blends. For the beginner it is best to start with relatively simple comparisons of three to four coffees, with no more than three to four tasters. The equipment necessary to begin refining your coffee palate is as close as the kitchen for most coffeelovers, and the process is fairly simple.

• A Coffee-Lover's Guide to Cupping •

For a tasting of three coffees, using three tasters.

Nine 6-ounce cups
3 tablespoons *each* whole beans of 3 different coffees
1 quart cold fresh water
3 soup spoons
3 notepads and pens

1. *Organize yourself:* Line up 3 sets of 3 cups, one set per taster, within close proximity of a sink. Access to a sink is important because tasting requires the spitting out of the coffee and the frequent rinsing of your spoon. Even the most avid coffee addict will flame out in a mass of caffeine-laden smoke and dust if a spittoon, or at least a kitchen sink, is not employed.

2. *Measure and grind* a tablespoon of beans for each person tasting, and finely grind them to the coarseness of cornmeal. Then take a teaspoon of the ground coffee and place it in the bottom of a cup. Repeat for each coffee you are tasting, making sure to wipe the grinder clean after each one. Note on a card which coffee is being tasted, and place it beneath your cups. (To be truly professional about your

tastings you should weigh the coffee rather than measuring it, as different coffees have different densities and therefore will take up more or less volume. If you choose to invest in a scale you should measure out 7¼ grams—the weight of a dime and a nickel—of whole-bean coffee.)

3. *Boil the water:* The water should be cold and allowed to run for a few seconds before filling the kettle, since water coming from the hot water heater or the water that comes immediately from the spout is sure to be unaerated. The water should also be free of foreign odors and tastes.

4. *Fill each cup* with the boiling water, in the order you will be tasting, just below the rim, returning the kettle to the burner if it begins to cool off too fast. On a notepad write down the names of the coffees in the order in which they were poured.

5. *Breaking the crust:* After allowing the coffees to cool for a minute or two, place your nose close to the cup, and, with the edge of the spoon, gently break the crust of grounds that has formed on the surface. (It's better to get a little coffee on your nose than to miss anything at this point.) "Breaking the crust" is considered one of the most important steps of tasting coffee, as it is your first impression of the coffee's full aroma.

Concentrate on keeping your impressions limited to the first couple of sniffs, since smelling for longer amounts of time will overwhelm your olfactory senses and make it impossible to get an accurate impression. Record your aromatic impressions, keeping the terms as precise as possible. For example, say "earthy" instead of "bad." (See our list of coffee vocabulary on page 25.) Limit each coffee to one or two of these concise terms rather than a half-dozen, which will only serve to confuse you later on. After noting the characteristic aroma of each cup, giving the spoon a

(*text continues on page 24*)

Spitting, Spittoons, and Other Traditions of the Coffee Trade

Some of these quaint customs are disappearing with the advent of labor laws, building codes, and a changing industry.

The culture and profession of cupping places severe demands on comportment and behavior. As in wine evaluation, the accuracy and neatness of one's expectorations are of paramount importance. In a professional cupping room three pieces of furniture figure prominently: the cupping table, the stool, and the spittoon. The table is round and rotates and is about three feet in diameter and four feet high; the cups are placed around the edge. The stool is high enough so that the edge of the table is about as high as the lower end of your sternum. The spittoon is about three feet high, hourglass in shape, with the top and bottom being about a foot in diameter and the center around four or five inches across. The spittoon should sit directly in front of you as you sit at the stool (or slightly to the side if you're a woman and wearing a skirt, which isn't likely if the cupping room is truly traditional). Tasting the coffee and then spitting it out should require as little motion as possible: either a slight lean backward or to the side. You should spit slightly off dead center so that you neither hit the upper wall of the spittoon nor the center, which would yield up an embarassing "plunk." Rotate the table with your left hand and spoon the coffee with your right. Taste each glass once and don't dawdle. Cupping coffee isn't for contemplative ninnies— you'll be kicked off your chair with a loud guffaw, the spittoon tumbling after.

Traditional coffee traders view themselves as men of action and practicality. Their offices, while often computerized, don't reveal a lot of silly self-indulgence. No fancy overstuffed furniture, no waiting rooms—just a lot of purposeful activity. But back to the spittoon, for through it much about the world of coffee is revealed.

Most professional tasting rooms have huge spittoons with an overall capacity of several gallons. They are usually mounted on plywood boards upon which are attached sturdy sofa casters—sturdy because a professional group of traders would never think of asking the junior employee to empty it until it was just brimming above its waist. That junior employee always has more important things to do, like roasting samples or fetching water to boil (the water spigot is always two floors down), or typing up an urgent contract. It is with great reluctance, then, that one of the senior traders will holler, "Hey, will someone empty this before it crawls out?!" At this point the junior will tense, flinch, and then scurry to the location of the spittoon.

The problem our coffee apprentice is faced with is that his senior partners have been so busy trading coffee for the past millenia (long before its discovery) that they've never stopped to notice that the floorboards are so worn that from certain angles they can see their competitors avidly trading, grinding, slurping, and spitting below them. (All credible coffee traders have traditionally rented office space adjacent to one another, invariably in the cheapest, most poorly kept building in town, the presence of a good neighborhood bar and grill influencing their decision greatly.) Junior then has to roll a brimful spittoon weighing slightly less than a sack of cement over rotting floorboards, out of the office, into the elevator, to the other floor where the men's room is, and then into a stall where he must judiciously wrestle the teetering mass of saliva, coffee grounds, and cigar butts slowly into the can. Such is the training and preparation of our future coffee traders. Not that coffee traders, in general, don't know coffee inside out. It's hard to imagine a group of professionals who know more about what they do, or show it less, than coffee brokers.

rinse after each, you may return to one you particularly liked, but at this point refrain from stirring, since the grounds are in the process of settling, and each cup should be brewed at the same strength.

6. *Slurp and spray:* When the coffees have cooled to a point at which they can be tasted without scalding the tongue, or slightly hotter than lukewarm, taste the coffee by dipping your spoon in it and slurping the coffee from the spoon's edge. When you make this noise you should be spraying the inside of your mouth with the coffee. The purpose of this is twofold: you are covering the entire tongue with the liquid so that each part can assess the tastes, and you are reaching the back of the mouth, which allows the nasal passages to assess the aroma again.

Different parts of the tongue will bring you different taste sensations: the back of the tongue tells you about the bitterness or acidity of the coffee; the sides of the tongue are sensitive to any staleness; and the tip of the tongue will note any specific flavors. The true taste analysis will come with the second slurping of the coffee, as the first generally clears your palate of the flavor of the previous coffee.

• *Acidity, Flavor, Body* •

You should be paying close attention to these three qualities: acidity, flavor, and body. Acidity is, in fine coffee, a pleasant sharpness. It is what adds life to the cup, accenting the characteristic flavor of a particular coffee. While a coffee low in acidity can result in a pleasant-tasting "mellow," or "soft," cup of coffee, the complete lack of acidity will leave the coffee tasting flat, or "dead," and will produce a lifeless cup. *Flavor* is the perception of the aromatic elements once the coffee is in the mouth, but in some cases it is also used to convey any specific taste that is present in the coffee, such as "nutty," "spicy," or "musty." *Body* is the impression of weight and texture that coffee leaves in the mouth, which leads it to be described in terms such as "rough" or "watery." Body is easiest to analyze in a full-strength brew, and should be assessed by working the coffee tactilely through the mouth.

THE VOCABULARY OF COFFEE

Certain characteristics are easy to distinguish even for the beginning taster, such as the difference between natural and washed coffees, and between high-grown and low-grown coffees. You will notice after directly comparing coffees that relatively small differences will be brought out in the cup. However, in order to fully utilize the cupping experience, and to even approach your own definition of the perfect cup of coffee, you need a vocabulary that describes these differences. It is therefore essential that you acquaint yourself with a standard glossary of terms before setting out to cup. I have included a small sampling of terms adapted from Ted Lingle's *Coffee Cupper's Handbook* (published by the Coffee Development Group, Washington, D.C.) and the cupping chart from I. & M. Smith (pty.), Ltd., but keep in mind that the more you cup, the more references you will have, and the easier it will be to distinguish the varietal characteristics.

» *Acidity* A measure of the acid content of the liquid; in fine coffees acidity results in a pleasant sharpness. Not to be associated with the genuinely sour taste of inferior coffees.

» *Aftertaste* The sensation of brewed coffee vapors released after swallowing. Characteristics will range from carbony to chocolaty, spicy to turpeny.

» *Aroma* The sensation of the gases released from brewed coffee; may be described as ranging from fruity to herby.

» *Bitter* Perceived by the back of the tongue and characterized by solutions of quinine, caffeine, and other alkaloids; usually caused by over-roasting.

» *Bland* Perceived by the sides of the tongue and ranging in taste from "soft" to neutral. Found often in washed arabica coffees such as Guatemalan Low Grown.

» *Body* Associated with mouthfeel and texture, this should be a strong, full, pleasant characteristic; see *mouthfeel*.

» *Bouquet* The total aromatic profile, resulting from compounds in the fragrance, aroma, and aftertaste.

» *Caramelly* A common aromatic sensation; reminiscent of candy or syrup.

» *Carbony* A common aromatic sensation in dark-roasted coffees, reminiscent of a burnt substance.

» *Chocolaty*   A common aromatic sensation in a brew's aftertaste, reminiscent of unsweetened chocolate or vanilla.

» *Dead*   See *flat.*

» *Delicate*   Related to *mellow;* characterized by a fragile, subtle flavor; perceived by the tip of the tongue. Found in washed New Guinea arabica coffee.

» *Dirty*   An unclean smell or taste that can be specific, such as sourness or mustiness, or a more generalized taint that reminds one of eating dirt.

» *Earthy*   See *dirty.*

» *Flat*   Used when describing bouquet to denote a lack of strong perceptions in fragrance, aroma, and aftertaste; also called *dead.*

» *Flavor*   The experience of aromatics once the coffee is in the mouth.

» *Fragrance*   The aromatic sensations inhaled by sniffing; can be described as ranging from sweetly floral to sweetly spicy.

» *Fruity*   An aromatic sensation reminiscent of citrus fruit or berries.

» *Grassy*   Used to describe an odor and/or taste in some coffees that is reminiscent of a freshly mown lawn, with an accompanying astringency like that of green grass.

» *Harsh*   A hard, raspy, often caustic flavor sometimes described as "rioy."

» *Lifeless*   See *thin.*

» *Mellow*   A rounded, smooth taste, characteristically lacking in acidity.

» *Mild*   Refers to a coffee that lacks any overriding characteristic, either pleasant or unpleasant.

» *Mouthfeel*   The tactile sensations the coffee produces on your palate.

» *Muddy*   A dull, indistinct, and thickish flavor that can be caused by the grounds being agitated.

» *Musty* A flavor that often occurs due to poor storage or lack of sufficient drying, aging, or overheating. In aged coffees mustiness is not necessarily undesirable.

» *Nutty* An aromatic sensation that is released as a brew is swallowed; reminiscent of roasted nuts.

» *Neutral* A flavor characteristic that is desirable in good blenders. Used to denote a lack of any strong flavors.

» *Rich* Used when describing bouquet to denote intense perceptions of fragrance, aroma, and aftertaste.

» *Rioy* A somewhat grainy or starchy taste, like potato soup in texture.

» *Rough* Characterized by a parched sensation on the tongue, related to sharp, salty taste sensations.

» *Rubbery* Caused when fruit is allowed to partially dry while still on the tree, this is a fault that gives beans the character of burnt rubber. It is found mostly in dry-processed **robustas,** not **arabicas.**

» *Soft* The absence of the parched sensation on the tongue; related to bland.

» *Sour* Related to over-acidity; a sharp, biting flavor, often from underripe beans.

» *Spicy* An aromatic and taste perception reminiscent of spices.

» *Sweet* Free of any harshness.

» *Taint* A chemical change in the bean brought about by any number of internal or external changes, which results in a change in the coffee's flavor.

» *Thin* Related to underbrewing, resulting in a coffee lacking in any acidity; also referred to as *lifeless.*

» *Turpeny* Tasting like turpentine smells.

» *Watery* Caused by the wrong water-to-coffee ratio, which results in the low level of oils in the coffee. This is mouthfeel.

» *Wild* A gamey flavor often associated with Ethiopian coffees.

» *Winey* Reminiscent of a well-matured red wine; characterized by a full-bodied, smooth coffee. Often found in Kenyan and Yemeni coffees.

≫ DECAFFEINATED COFFEE ≪

Decaffeinated coffee has been processed prior to roasting in order to remove 96 to 98 percent of the caffeine originally present in the beans. All decaffeination processes disrupt the physical and chemical structure of the coffee bean, and therefore change the flavor of the coffee. It is a common misconception that the more "natural" the process, the better the coffee will taste—this is certainly not the case. And while there has been much hysteria generated with regard to solvent-processed decaffeinated coffee, the evidence is slim to suggest that these products are actually in any way unhealthful. Ecologically, however, the solvent, methylene chloride, could present a very different story. There is evidence that it is harmful to the ozone layer, and its use worldwide will likely be banned by the end of the century. In any event, several other means of decaffeination are available. Following is a brief overview of current decaffeination processes.

One basic process is used to decaffeinate coffee: coffee is warmed and rinsed with a solvent several times to remove as much caffeine as possible. The coffee is then dried, and the solvent is removed.

The solvent of choice is methylene chloride (CH_3Cl), and when the solvent is used in direct contact with the beans it is called *direct method* or *direct methylene chloride process*. Many people who taste and evaluate coffees professionally feel that this method produces the best-tasting coffee. The reason is that methylene chloride specifically adheres to and dissolves the caffeine but very little else that is found in the coffee. Other solvents will dissolve many of the important components that contribute to the coffee's flavor. KVW, which I refer to quite a few times, is a company in Hamburg that has been processing decaffeinated coffee via methylene chloride for a number of years and has gained a reputation for doing it better than most. A variation on the direct method uses water to rinse the coffee. The same water is then mixed with methylene chloride, removing the caffeine from the water but leaving the other components of the coffee in. The water, which is used over and over again, develops high concentrations of these flavor components and theoretically then does not remove any of these components from subsequent batches of coffee to be decaffeinated. This process is usually referred to as the *indirect method*. The problem with the indirect method is that some consumer advocates claim that the coffee is still exposed to small amounts of methylene chloride. Many roasters and retailers call the indirect method *European water process* or simply *water process*. This should not be confused with the Swiss Water™ Process, which is a patented process of the Swiss Water Decaf Division, Nabob Foods Ltd.

Concerns regarding methylene chloride have resulted in a number of tests. When inhaled by laboratory rats in high concentrations methylene chloride as found to cause cancer. However, ingestion did not produce the same results. In late 1989 the FDA determined that the lifetime carcinogenic risk from methylene chloride was less than one in a million for those consumers preferentially consuming large amounts of decaffeinated coffee. Methylene chloride, it should be noted, is an expensive solvent that boils at 103° F. Because coffee is roasted at close to 400° F and brewed at over 200° F, it is unlikely that more than a few molecules of the stuff remain in a brewed cup of coffee. Aside from its volatility, the high cost of the solvent and the health hazard its presence might pose motivates the processor to recover as much of the solvent as possible.

Another fact to keep in mind about methylene chloride is that it takes extremely high concentrations (up to 100,000 times as much as could be found in a cup brewed from *unroasted* coffee) to produce cancer in laboratory animals. The Swiss Water process has become a popular alternative for the health-conscious. This process uses nothing but activated carbon filters and water to decaffeinate the green beans. The beans are soaked in water to remove the caffeine, which is water soluble, and then dried, cleaned and bagged.

To address problems regarding flavor absorption and consistency, Swiss Water has integrated many changes into its original process. The water used to decaffeinate the green coffee is "flavor charged", literally saturated with the water soluble components of the green coffee, including caffeine, sugars, and other flavor compounds. This water is next decaffeinated through carbon filters for use on all subsequent batches of beans. The use of "flavor-charged" water, as well as recent innovations in reducing the amount of water used in the process, has led to vast improvements in the taste of coffees decaffeinated with Swiss Water. Since the opening of the Vancouver, B.C. facilities, Swiss Water has also done a fine job of catering to the specialty industry, offering total decaffeination and substantial marketing support.

These coffees are more expensive than either direct or indirect processed decafs. And, because retailers can charge a premium for name brand recognition and association with health and environmental issues, there is the possibility of unethical behavior. When the words "water processed" appear on bags or bins of coffee beans, it is common for retailers and consumers to assume that the product has been decaffeinated without the use of chemicals. Since all decaffeinated processes, even those which use chemical agents such as methylene chloride and ethyl acetate, begin by using water or steam to open up the bean, technically all decaffeinated coffees can be labeled "water processed".

Natural process decaffeinated coffees are those processed

by methods which use a solvent, other than water, that occurs in nature. The *ethyl acetate process*, and the *supercritical* CO_2 *(carbon dioxide)* process both fall into this category. It is felt that these two solvents dissolve less of the flavor components of the coffee than does water, while still removing the caffeine. ("Supercritical" CO_2, by the way, is carbon dioxide gas that has been pressurized enough to convert it to a liquid state.)

As the CO_2 method gains familiarity and consistency, it could replace the direct method as the industry standard. While many in the industry still prefer chemical decaf, Swiss Water has gained tremendous ground in quality improvements, and now holds a large share of the specialty decaffeinated market. I have taken experienced roasters to the Vancouver plant for blind cuppings, and they have repeatedly chosen the Swiss Water decaf coffees over coffees decaffeinated with other processes.

FLAVORED COFFEE

Flavored coffees originally were a way for wholesalers to use less-expensive coffees when coffee prices escalated in the early 1970s. The acceptance of these coffees was much greater than anticipated, however, particularly among those who were not familiar with specialty whole-bean coffee. Much to the discomfort of many coffee-lovers like myself, flavored coffees have flourished.

Coffee purists will be disappointed to learn that from the time coffee was first consumed as an infusion of the roasted beans, it was often flavored with spices such as cardamom, nutmeg, cinnamon, and black pepper and also with citrus rinds. In the Middle East, ground nuts were mixed with the coffee before brewing. Many of the flavors we might think of as exotic, unusual, and new are variations on flavor combinations that are as old as coffee itself (this doesn't make them desirable, just old).

Basically, coffee is flavored by a mixture of flavoring and a "carrier" that is applied to the coffee just after it has been roasted and has cooled to about 100°. At this point the beans are able to absorb the mixture; after they cool, the flavoring is "locked" in the whole beans until the coffee is ground and brewed. The carrier is a non-toxic, neutral compound (secret in most formulations), which allows the flavoring to spread evenly over the warm beans.

Flavorings come in three basic varieties: natural, nature-identic, and artificial. Natural flavors are derived from the actual material that has the desired flavor; for example, natural orange flavor comes from oranges. Nature-identic flavors are chemicals that are artificially produced but that have the exact chemical structure of the naturally occurring chemicals. It is usually possible to produce much more concentrated flavorings in the nature-identic form than in the natural mode. There are some flavors, such as the flavor of coffee, that are not composed of one single flavor but of many components. These flavors are the hardest to imitate. Artificial flavors mimic the sensation caused by the desired flavor, but are artificially derived and chemically different from their natural counterparts. These flavorings are usually the cheapest, but they are also the least similar to the flavoring they are intended to imitate.

≫ LEARNING THE LANGUAGE ≪

The best way to think of coffee's flavor is as that of a roasted fruit seed. Aside from being exactly what it is, the phrase brings to mind the two primary components of coffee's flavor: fruit substances and the by-products of the roasting process. The fruit flavors are like those that eonophiles refer to when they talk about aroma; that is, the properties that we taste and smell that nature has already installed in the grape or coffee bean. Second are the roasting by-products, which can be thought of as the "bottle bouquet" of coffee: the compounds that appear due to human intervention.

Just as wine has no single flavor compound that gives rise to a winelike taste, there is no integral "coffee flavor." There are, in fact, hundreds of compounds in coffee that give it flavor and aroma. These components vary from one coffee to another. Certain coffees have two or three times more kinds of aromatic oils than others; generally these more complex coffees are considered better by professional tasters.

Within the first category of coffee flavors—those that are already in the roasted bean—there are some subdivisions: fruit acids, mineral salts, and some aromatic compounds that survive the roasting process but are unlocked from the confines of the bean's cellular structure by it.

One of the more inexplicable characteristics of coffee is its fruitiness. Coffee, with its dark color and deep, intense aroma, does not immediately call to mind lemon, cherries, or grapes. Yet many of the simple organic acids found in these fruits are also found in brewed coffee. And as any winemaker will tell you, each of these organic acids has its own characteristic pucker. Malic tends to a mellower note than citric, for example, and fumaric is not as pleasant as either. When found in the taste of a particular coffee these organic acids add high notes of a pleasant sharpness and bite. They also balance a heavy-bodied coffee and accentuate delicate aromatics in lighter brews.

Organic acids have nothing to do with the slow, unpleasant sourness found in some coffees. That taste is often due to beans that have fermented, or have gone sour, before they've been roasted.

It is difficult to describe the standard by which coffee is determined to be good. I think of good coffees as ones that, despite their processing, roasting, and brewing, somehow transport the scent and flavor of the land, air, and water of their origin. Some coffees, when you taste them, transport you back to their birthplace.

• *The Taste of Coffee* •

If coffee does not have a single taste or flavor and if there is no compound or molecule that can be isolated as the flavor source, then where does coffee's flavor come from? Coffee's flavor comes simultaneously from its aroma—as vapors after the coffee is brewed—and from the water-soluble organic and inorganic natural chemical components that make up its taste. A mixture of petroleum distillates and simple alcohols, warmed and poured into an opaque mug, was identified by several people as having the aroma of coffee in one study in which participants were not allowed to see the beverage they were drinking. There are many simple hydrocarbons resulting from the roasting of coffee that could account for this result. But there is a lot more to the flavor chemistry of coffee than simple hydrocarbons.

The flavor of coffee comes from many different sources within the bean. First there is the woody, fibrous structure of the bean, which, as it is roasted, will oxidize into bitter, carbonaceous compounds. Next there are the methyl-xanthines: caffeine, theophylline, and theobromine, of which caffeine is the best known. These are all methylated derivatives of xanthine, which is a dioxypurine, and in coffee this contributes to the bitterness. Aromatic oils add to the aroma of coffee and to its flavor; that is, the experiencing of the aromatics as the coffee is being drunk. Mineral salts and organic acids also contribute taste: mineral salts give the organic acids a different tone and depth.

Coffee's flavor is not due only to the compounds in it, however, but also to the degree to which they've reacted since the coffee was brewed. Many coffees, particularly those high in acid, actively change in chemical makeup in the first few minutes after they are brewed. For this reason, most coffees sold to restaurants are specifically blended to remain consistent even after sitting on the burner for an hour or more.

Over the years, a language has been developed to describe the various sensations encountered while drinking coffee. These include *earthy, rubbery, grassy, winey* and *acidy* (see "The Vocabulary of Coffee," page 25). The experiences that these words describe are probably not what the uninitiated coffee taster would expect. For instance, according to one wall chart published by I. & M. Smith, Ltd., and prominent in coffee-tasting rooms around the world, *acidy* is described as "a sharp and pleasing characteristic."

The nuances developed in the professional lexicon, however, are not shared by those coffee drinkers who, while they may love coffee, are not involved with it professionally. When over thirty coffee drinkers (not professionals) who drink coffee every day that they consider at least "very good" were asked to identify five flavors they associate with coffee, more than 80 percent could not name any. Despite this, most said that they drink coffee for the "flavor." When asked what constitutes a good-flavored coffee, most of the people surveyed referred to characteristics that would be classified as having to do with "mouthfeel," that is, a coffee's body, or its tactual feel in the mouth. Primary among their descriptions was the word *richness,* which, although a term held in low regard by many professional coffee tasters, usually means "full bodied." To nonprofessionals it also seems to mean a coffee with an abundance of aroma and flavor, although both remain indefinable.

In addition to the presence of compounds in coffee that give it taste and flavor, there are specific components (often the aromatic oils themselves, among other things) that give coffee its body, or mouthfeel. This viscosity of coffee is what most people surveyed found appealing about it.

The degree to which it possessed this attribute seemed to be the primary determinant in judging a particular coffee aesthetically.

• *The Taste for Coffee* •

More mysterious than the exploration of *what* we perceive as the flavor of coffee is the question of *why* people find coffee so likable. Certainly the aroma of warm hydrocarbons is not appealing. Nor is the idea of quaffing several different types of methylxanthines in solution. Coffee is drunk in many forms, each producing its own flavor result; wide ranges of quality are also consumed, seemingly all with some pleasure. Can we account for coffee's popularity solely on the basis of its mildly addicting caffeine content? If that were true people would probably find No-Doz more convenient.

I do not believe that people are unaware of taste. Rather, the problem resides in language, and the difficulty of communicating in words what a coffee tastes like.

Language is not just a tool for communicating to others, but a way of storing and comparing information from different events. We do not simply store up our life experiences in a jumble of impressions; instead we flag our experiences with key words that unfold into complete memories as we need them.

Without words that tap into similar experiences and perceptions it is impossible to describe an event to another person who has not had the same experience. Green-coffee brokers find it difficult to select a coffee that a particular customer will like unless they both speak the same language. Until I know what customer A means when he says "I need an acidic, clean blender, sort of sweet," I won't be able to send the right sample. Likewise, when visiting farms, the more specific an idea I have of what my customers need, the more information I can give the farmer. Based on that information, a farmer can grow and process his coffee in ways that will alter its flavor.

More could be done to improve the taste of coffees if coffee drinkers were able to verbalize their preferences. For instance, *The Coffee Cupper's Handbook,* by Ted R. Lingle, addresses the interactions between mineral salts, organic acids, sweet-tasting carbohydrates (as caramelized sugars), amino acids, and by-products of the roasting process. The presence of mineral salts can increase the sweetness of sugars and reduce the sourness of acids. Each of the mineral salts also has a characteristic flavor of its own. By adjusting the soil chemistry and processing techniques at a coffee farm the amounts of these various compounds in brewed coffee can be carefully controlled. But the consumer has no tools to express what is appealing and what isn't. Further, the aggressive marketing and advertising of large commercial firms only confuse the issue by insisting that relatively mediocre (at best) coffee is rich, full bodied, and robust.

Only an awareness of flavor can lead to informed decisions at the retail level, to the demise of hype, and to the perfect cup.

A COFFEE-LOVER'S GUIDE TO THE WORLD OF COFFEE

Note. For information on washed and unwashed coffees, see page 169. For information on specific estates, see the section beginning on page 176.

The way a coffee tastes depends a lot on the soil, climate, and cultivation methods involved. All of these phenomena tend to have regional generalities, so the coffees of Central America, for instance, have more in common with each other than with those of Brazil or Africa. Indonesian coffees too, have similar characteristics despite the varying ways in which the farmers of the different regions process them. Another coffee-growing area of the world is the range of mountains and hills that runs from northwestern Yemen—with a brief interruption across the Red Sea and the Gulf of Aden—through Ethiopia, Kenya, Tanzania, Malawi, and Zimbabwe. A similar range unites Central America, Guatemala, Honduras, El Salvador, Nicaragua, Costa Rica, and Panama to the coffees of Colombia, Ecuador, and Peru. Brazilian coffee, the most plentiful in the world, defines its own regional character with its own combination of processing methods, climate, soil, and trees. Finally, the island coffees seem to define a region united only by the great distances between them. The coffees of Jamaica, Kona, and Tahiti are, I like to think, similar to each other in mildness, balance, and a slightly spicy aroma.

❧ **BRAZIL** Quality is not generally high even though production is mainly *arabica,* because the processing methods are generally very crude and produce natural, or unwashed coffee. These beans are much in demand as a neutral coffee for blending purposes. Brazils are classified by an elaborate process using port names, estate names, bean types, and so on, but mostly according to the bean sizes and grades typically accepted by large roasters (such as "Folger's B").

Lately, certain farmers, shippers, and importers have been seeking to market better-quality Brazils, both washed and dry processed. Ideally, a good Brazil is medium bodied and very mild in acidity. The best Brazils have a complex and balanced aroma and a taste and mouthfeel that is sweet and lingering. A dry spiciness that includes hints of allspice and cloves is usually a characteristic of good Brazils.

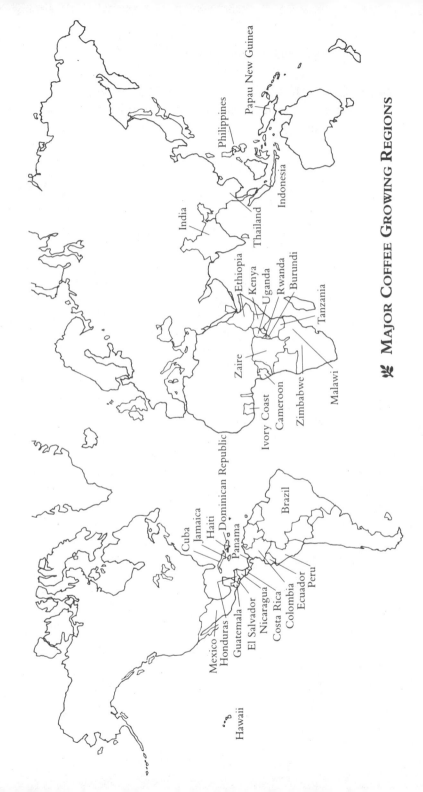

🌿 MAJOR COFFEE GROWING REGIONS

❧ COLOMBIA The two exportable grades are Supremo and Excelso; Supremos are generally larger than Excelsos. There are several specific rules about how many of this-sized bean and how many of that-sized bean can be exported as a Supremo as opposed to an Excelso, but most exporters ignore these rules as convenience and economics dictate, which is most of the time. Colombian coffee is one of the most consistently good coffees produced in the world today. The fact that there are 12 million 154-pound bags produced every year makes the quality of Colombian coffee even more impressive. The marketing of Colombian coffee has been very effective. By dint of their Juan Valdez advertising program, an extensive rebate/price protection plan, and a comprehensive advertising-allowance program offered to roasters, the Colombians have succeeded in making their product and logo one of the most recognized in the world, particularly in the United States, where everyone *knows* that Colombian coffee is the "richest."

While Colombian coffee is good, however, it is certainly not the world's best, any more than any other very good coffee is. Many experienced tasters feel that its flavor is not as clear and bright as others and that it has neither the complex elegance of a good Guatemalan coffee nor the pungently heavy body of a good Indonesian.

Nonetheless, Colombian coffee is noted for its good acidity, balanced with medium body and full aroma. Perhaps what most distinguishes it is a sweet, caramelly taste and mouthfeel, which makes it an excellent "self drinker" (unblended), although it can muddy and confuse a carefully constructed blend.

❧ COSTA RICA produces washed *arabica* coffee with excellent acidity and good body. The beans are generally large, flat, and uniform in size.

Costa Rican coffee is very good, but in my opinion almost too good. Prissily balanced and sweetly smooth, like a very pretty face, Costa Rican coffee can bore you with its goodness. The exceptions, though, are excellent. A few of the Terazus, such as the Dotas, have a wildly spicy, complex taste and very heavy body. The Bellavistas, from the Tres Rios region, are at once elegant and rough. The La Minita, from Tarrazu, is the most carefully processed coffee in the world and offers a taste that is as focused as a laser, the kind of taste that many pros feel Jamaican coffee *used* to have.

CUBA produces coffee quite typical of the Caribbean region, rather flat and best suited for dark roasts.

EL SALVADOR A large amount of production is in milds, but there is a quantity of "Strictly High Grown" that is to be noted for its medium acidity, body, and a mild, sweet taste. Most exports are round, full-bodied coffees used widely in blending. Salvadors offer particularly good balance to espresso blends: just enough roughness and imperfection to add interest.

ETHIOPIA Most of the coffee produced is still gathered from wild trees, resulting in natural, unwashed coffees. Ethiopian coffees are often noted for having a "wild" flavor to them, and are generally thought of as highly exotic. Ultimately they are very acidic and possess a sharp, tangy quality with thick-bodied liquors. The flavors are sometimes vegetative or earthy in nature. Many Ethiopian coffees, however, may lack acidity and have undesirable flavor qualities. The most consistent is genuine Harrar, graded by size into "Longberry" and "Shortberry"; the coffee has full body and an earthy complex aroma of cinnamon, new-mown grass, and ripe strawberries. The trouble is that almost all the "Harrar" you see in a store is usually lower-grade Ethiopian coffee that has been upgraded by the exporter or importer ("upgrading" in this case involves the competent, but certainly not fastidious, use of a stencil and some ink). If you didn't pay a lot, it wasn't Harrar. If you paid a lot but after drinking it you don't understand why you paid a lot, it wasn't Harrar, either.

🌿 **GUATEMALA** The "Strictly Hard Bean" grade produces long bluish beans that can be aromatic, lively, and acidy but perfectly balanced, with a soft, mild flavor and a heavy body. Famous regional coffees include Coban, Huehuetenango, Antigua, Atitlan, and Freihanes. Guatemalan coffee has a distinctive smokiness that is at once subtle and unforgettable—many coffee pros (including this writer) identify Guatemalan as their favorite.

🌿 **HAITI** produces both washed and unwashed coffees, which vary in quality. The high-grown beans are heavy bodied, mellow, and flavorful, while the low-growns tend to be musty and poor. This coffee, and coffee from the neighboring Dominican Republic, is soft beaned and great for roasting dark, developing a sweet, hard-candy taste without the bitterness of many dark-roast coffees.

🌿 **HAWAII** Kona, the coffee-producing district of Hawaii, contains ideal growing conditions for *arabica*. The large, flat beans can attain a superb aroma, with a hint of cinnamon and cloves. They are medium bodied but have a buttery characteristic. At their typical quality they are equal to most ordinary milds, and for the money do not measure up to many of the regional or estate-grown Central Americans. Given the price this coffee demands it is surprising that so many people buy it, but such is the romance of Kona coffee.

⚘ HONDURAS produces coffee widely used in blending, most of it washed, the best of which has good acidity but indistinct flavor and a very mild iodine-like taste (called *hard* in the coffee trade).

⚘ INDIA produces both washed and unwashed coffee. Monsoon Malabar is one of the best Indian coffees and one of the most consistently available aged coffees in the world. The coffee has a deep, full mouthfeel and body with a complex and powerfully spicy aroma and very little acidity. Notes of cinnamon and a strong hint of cedar characterize this coffee.

⚘ INDONESIA Java produces a small amount of washed high-grown *arabicas,* which ideally are spicy and strong-flavored, with low acidity and a full body; Sumatra produces unwashed coffees that are unusually heavy bodied and can achieve an intense and exotic flavor; a deep, cellary mustiness characterizes most of Sumatra's coffee and is thought by many to be desirable. Some Sumatra will have a touch of acidity and be very clean and straightforward, but also with deep, earthy body. Consistency seems to be the greatest lack in this coffee.

Javas, on the other hand, being washed and more carefully farmed than their cousins the Sumatras, are also very full bodied but have a balancing acidity and a milky or creamy mouthfeel and aftertaste.

⚘ JAMAICA Most famous for its Blue Mountain district, which at its best produces coffees that are acidy, aromatic, and full bodied. This coffee used to be one of the best in the world. Production is very small, and most of the coffee sold under the label Blue Mountain is nothing of the sort. Two other exportable grades are a good-quality high-grown known as High Mountain Supreme, and a nondescript low-grown called Prime Washed. In the past ten years I have not tasted a single Jamaican coffee worth (in my opinion) one-fifth the asking price. The Jamaican coffee industry, in league with non-Jamaican investors, have milked the legend of Jamaican coffee dry while expanding the Blue Mountain region with cynical indifference. The result is a coffee that, in a blind tasting, would be difficult to distinguish from a medium-grade coffee from any other coffee-producing country in the world. Still, a lot of Jamaican coffee gets sold at very, very high prices. The explanation? P. T. Barnum had the best one I can think of. "There's a sucker born every minute."

❧ KENYA produces washed *arabica,* much of it grown at high elevations and yielding a sharply acidic coffee with an intense flavor, very fragrant and floral. Prime Kenya coffees are clean and bright, with solid body and a sometimes "winey taste"; at their poorest they take on a sour note.

❧ MALAWI produces a small amount of fine-quality *arabica* similar in cup to the Kenyas but perhaps with a little less refinement and a touch more body.

❧ MEXICO The beans are large, with a prominent ridge, and produce very attractive roasts. The crème de la crème have medium acidity, a sweet, smooth body, and a flavor with a hint of roasted hazelnuts. They make an excellent brew by themselves when they are well balanced and clean. They are good blenders, letting the characteristics of more strongly aromatic coffees come through without muddying them.

❧ NICARAGUA Production is of neutral, washed beans used extensively in blending. The high-growns may exhibit good acidity and a mild flavor. Coffees from Matgalpa, Jinotega, and Nuevo Segovia rank with the best coffees in the world. Like Antiguas but without the smokiness, Nicaraguan coffees have an elusive cognac flavor.

✣ **PANAMA** All production is in high-quality coffee, "Strictly Hard Bean" grade, which has good acidity, is heavy bodied, and has a mild flavor. "Bouquete" is mild and balanced, famous for its smooth, sweet character.

✣ **PAPUA NEW GUINEA** produces both *arabica* and *robusta*. The high-grown washed *arabica* is of good quality. The Sigri estate produces particularly sweet, full-bodied coffee with an unobtrusive but almost perfectly balanced "coffee" taste. Coffees bearing the Koban mark are also very good. New Guineas are sleepers in specialty coffee, and may have the potential to be among the best.

✣ **PERU** can produce some excellent high-grown coffee with good acidity and body, and mild flavor, with nothing to distinguish it from any other coffee. This country *could* produce great coffee, but its economic infrastructure makes producing anything at all a miracle. Peru also produces some of the world's worst *arabica* coffee.

✣ **VENEZUELA** produces mainly coffees for blending, the quality of which varies considerably. Venezuela produces both light-bodied, delicate coffees and full-bodied mellow coffees. The coffees are shipped from the port of Maracaibo and are sometimes referred to by that name.

Venezuelan coffee, also referred to as "Tachiras," is often rebagged into Colombian sacks with the knowledge and consent of the importer and the roaster.

✣ **YEMEN** produces natural coffee, commonly referred to as Mocha, which at its best yields a unique bitter, winey cup with a hint of cherries. Most Mochas do not approach this famous standard, however, even the ones that are genuine—which are very few indeed, as the vast majority of beans sold as Yemeni are actually Ethiopian. Sometimes, though, coffees sold as either genuine Mattari or Sunani are quite good.

❧ **ZAIRE** produces mainly *robustas,* except for some high-grown *arabicas* out of the Kivu and Ituri districts, which have an excellent balance of acidity, body, and flavor.

❧ **ZIMBABWE** produces coffee similar to Kenya's but with less "wineyness" and more body.

ROASTING

In the area of food and drink coffee stands alone, without similar models to describe the phenomena that bring it from farm to cup. Wine, for instance, is one of many fermented alcoholic beverages including beer, and they can all claim kinship when asked about their pedigree. The processing of cocoa, the other roasted bean, departs radically from that of coffee once both escape the inquisition of roasting.

Coffee, in fact, needs a great deal of human intervention before it becomes palatable. The final decoction resembles the raw material not in the least. Coffee is desirable only as the shadow it casts in liquid.

Coffee, too, is unique in the relatively long shelf life of the raw natural product. Before roasting, some coffees may be kept for years. Indeed, many coffees improve with aging. (Although the concept of aging is a bit more complex than many suppose.)

Green coffee beans are essentially the seeds of the coffee tree. In this state there are only subtle clues of the aroma and character that will appear later in the cup. These seeds contain oils, waxes, fats, sugars, and complex polysaccharides, including starches and the woody material that makes up the structure of the bean. Before roasting, the integrity of the cell walls of the bean prevents the dissolu-

Roasting Machine

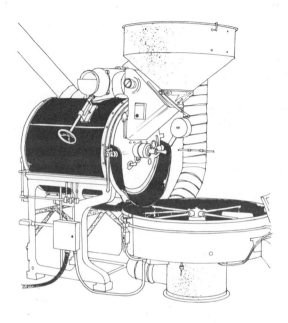

tion of the flavor components present. The first thing that roasting does is break down the coffee bean's cellular structure allowing for the escape of aromatic oils and other flavor components. Brewed coffee is primarily an extraction of mineral salts, sugars, aromatic oils, and starches. A good percentage of these compounds is not present in green coffee, but is developed as the coffee is roasted. There are some substances, however, that are present in both green and roasted coffee, such as caffeine, which decreases in concentration during the roasting process, and adds to the bitter flavor of coffee. Roasting coffee, then, is a dialectic of destruction and creation. The integrity of the bean progressively disintegrates as the woody structure of the bean is rent apart, and flavors either develop or are made available through this process.

It is the job of the coffee roaster to understand this double edge of the roasting process, knowing that with each development of a flavor component another is being lost forever. Having a distinct idea of which flavors to keep and to bring out and which to cast off is the key to roasting with a consistent and appreciable style. The economic necessity of optimizing value is also essential. A coffee without a lot of varietal character ideally may be dark roasted, for instance, because all coffees are capable of developing the flavors found in dark-roasted coffees. This is not to say that high-quality coffee doesn't make a difference in dark roasting. There are roasters who successfully utilize darker-roasting techniques while maintaining the distinct characteristics of each coffee's origins, but you will find that their success depends heavily on the quality of beans that they use.

Roasting may also be thought of as an art form (for more on the art of coffee roasting, see page 86). Experienced roasters can control quite meticulously the flavors they choose to reveal and those they may wish to conceal. A good coffee roaster also needs to have a keen sense of the environment. Humidity, temperature, and the specific history of a given lot of coffee can all affect the outcome of a roast and dramatically alter its progress. During hot, sultry summer months, for instance, coffee beans may go into a roaster 20° warmer and in a much softer state than they would in the winter.

• The Stages of Roasting •

Coffee roasting proceeds in a series of definite stages. The first involves the heating of the bean to slightly less than the boiling point of water. During this stage the beans become greener and swell a bit. As the heated water within

(*text continues on page 52*)

The Machine Behind The Bean

If you've been into a coffeehouse that does its own roasting, chances are you spied a large metal contraption somewhere in the near vicinity. It most likely had a large pipe leading outside, and perhaps was spilling forth beans like lava. All most of us need to know is that the machine is in operation on a regular basis, so we're getting the freshest possible coffee. More than one roaster, in fact, has been told "I want *that!*" by a customer pointing to the just-released batch. For those of you who liked to take apart everything when you were younger, here's what the inside of the machine looks like.

There are a number of roasters available for the small roaster-retailer today. Michael Sivetz, a guru to some roasters, has invented and patented his own machine (see the Kaladi Brothers profile, page 146). Carlo Di Ruocco uses wood roasting to obtain his famous espressos (see "Espresso Yourself," page 77). Here are two other roasters:

Stephen Diedrich used to design airplanes; now he designs coffee roasters. His father, Carl, designed and built the first Diedrich coffee roasters thirty years ago, for use on the family coffee plantation (see the interview with his brother Martin, page 122, for more on this historic coffee family). Today Steve has refined those original designs, and Diedrich Manufacturing Company offers several models to choose from. The machines operate by indirect heating, and rapid cooling with air.

Beans—any amount from ·one to fifty pounds in their most popular machine—are dropped into a solid high-carbon steel drum that rotates inside. The beans are roasted by a combination of hot air being drawn through the chamber, and the drum, which is heated from infrared heat coming off of ceramic fiber plates under the drum. While the beans are roasting, chaff that has flaked off the bean is collected and removed. When the beans are roasted to the desired color, they are released into a cooling bin, which has an agitator to keep the beans circulating. (The color of the beans is checked by a metal chute with a handle, which when pulled out is filled with beans.) A vacuum system draws cool air through the beans after they're released to cool them off quickly.

Probat Roastery Supply is another manufacturer of roasting equipment. Their technology extends to huge machines that can process coffee from green to ground, all by computer. Their less-overwhelming machinery appears in many retail outlets, however, and since they have been making roasting equipment since 1868, they know what they're doing. Probat machines work by heating air in a separate enclosed chamber and then passing it through the roasting drum. This drum contains special "vanes" that keep the beans circulating in a regular manner for even roasting. The substructure includes a chaff collector. When done, the beans are released and cooled in a large tray with a special stirring mechanism to keep them cooling evenly. A quenching device that sprays a quick blast of water onto the beans to quickly drop the temperature may also be used.

the bean becomes steam, however, the green color quickly dissipates and the bean will begin to audibly crack as the woody structure is disrupted by the escaping vapors. The second stage begins after most of the water has evaporated and the complex polysaccharides present in the bean cells are broken down into starches and finally sugars. These sugars then caramelize, partially contributing to the color of roasted coffee. This process is essentially one of tearing apart a molecular chain and building it back up in another pattern. As the second stage ends, additional complex proteins and organic acids are broken down into simpler substances. Aromatic oils present in the bean volatilize and boil toward the surface of the bean. During this third stage the beans develop an oily appearance. The expansion of these oils causes the second "crack" that the bean will undergo. After this period the roasting process proceeds much more quickly; many of the aromatics present will either vaporize entirely or break down into smaller component parts. Varietal qualities are lost during the last stages of roasting, and the characteristic French roast flavor becomes progressively stronger.

No matter how roasting is achieved, in what type of roasting apparatus, by what temperature, or for what length of time, a number of judgment calls are required before roasted coffee is produced. If roasting is done thoughtfully it takes into consideration which natural properties each coffee or blend of coffee possesses. Roasts range anywhere from semi-roast to French roast. "Full-city roast," a commonly used term, is the darkest roast one can achieve before the bean gets oily. In a full-city roast, the oil may just begin to bead on the surface of the bean.

• Roasting Styles •

Roasting style attempts to accentuate those qualities of the bean that the roaster feels are the most desirable. This will

Roasting Terminology

The roast given to most commercial or canned coffees in the United States is not much darker than a pale cinnamon color. This is an effort to reduce as much weight loss as possible, and therefore to make as much profit as possible. For anybody just beginning to explore the delights of specialty coffee, one of the first noticeable things is the variety of roasting styles that specialty coffee roasters and retailers use, and the plethora of names these roasts go by. The names of the different roasts are often derived from the drinking preferences of geographical areas, such as Italian, Viennese, New Orleans. Then there are terms such as *city roast, half-city roast,* and *full-city roast. Full-city* is a commonly used term in the industry, but unfortunately, it seems that every roaster has his or her own idea of what it means. In an effort to keep these terms straight I've compiled the ones I hear the most often and listed them from light to dark.

LIGHT ROASTS	MEDIUM ROASTS
Cinnamon	Full city
Half city	American
	Regular
	Breakfast

DARK ROASTS	DARKEST ROASTS
Continental	French
New Orleans	Italian
Vienna	Espresso

not always lead to the same result in the final product. Guatemalan Antigua, for instance, is a hard, highly acidic coffee. It can be roasted to a very dark degree and still retain its natural fruitiness and flavor, with just enough acid to give it sparkle. Another roaster might choose to revel in the acidity of this coffee, though, and roast it lighter. This degree of choice gives the roaster considerable latitude in framing the gifts nature has given each of the world's coffees. Sumatran coffees, on the other hand, are known for their velvety and voluptuous body and mild acidity. These characteristics encourage certain roasters to roast this coffee very little to maintain the fragile high notes; others are encouraged to go full bore, roasting it just short of dark and oily to take full advantage of its syrupy body. The results of each approach are valid, and (more important) tasty, but most everyone will prefer one over the other, and a few will adamantly dislike a particular style.

The burnt taste of darker roasts is commonly mistaken for higher quality simply because it is such an improvement over the under-roasted canned coffees the average consumer is used to. Dark roasts can be enjoyable, especially if one uses high-quality beans and proper storage methods, but one dark roast will taste pretty much the same as the next, if low-quality beans are used. Although I've stressed that coffee is capable of being interpreted in innumerable ways, once you get to a certain level of darkness, it would take a psychic to tell the difference. Something to be aware of: many coffee retailers charge higher prices for their dark roasts because of the weight loss incurred by dark roasting and the additional time this roast requires.

• *Local Tastes* •

Popular roasting styles seem to develop locally, and preferences, like most tastes in food, are dependent on what people are used to. Once a given "taste" in coffee takes hold in a geographic area or culture it is difficult to uproot. It has been suggested that dark roasts have become popular in areas where lower-quality coffees have traditionally been used. But this rule of thumb has many exceptions: really poor coffee beans break apart and begin to burn up in a dark roast, and many fine coffees, like the aforementioned Antiguas, can endure the rigors of dark roasting and come out intact.

Geographic location may also play a part in how a particular roast is referred to. Depending on where you are in the country, darker roasts may be referred to by a variety of names, including Continental, Vienna, and New Orleans roast. The darkest roast possible, which renders the beans almost black, is called Italian roast on the East Coast, and French roast on the West Coast (see the chart on page 53).

• *The Dark, the Light, and the Ugly* •

Coffee drinkers, in choosing a preferred roasting style, can increase their enjoyment of coffee immensely by looking for other flavors and nuances beyond the initial characteristics of the roast itself. Many "gourmets," for instance, particularly in the San Francisco area, reflexively associate the flavor of dark-roasted coffee with "high-quality" coffee. This approach not only leaves them vulnerable to charlatans willing to roast anything in a burlap sack, but cheats the reputable roaster of the opportunity to show them the special qualities a fine coffee develops when roasted to a particular degree.

The darkness or lightness of a roast is not the only factor a coffee roaster considers. The speed of a given roast also has a profound effect on the character of the final cup. Many commercial roasters have discovered that low-quality coffees, teeming with defects, can be smoothed considerably by roasting them very quickly in the presence of a great deal of quickly moving hot air. The latest developments in roasting technology have emphasized much faster roasting times, some promising to deliver roasted coffee in less than ninety seconds. Among these systems is the much-advertised "puff roasting" concept, which exposes the coffee beans to so much heat so quickly that the coffee behaves like popcorn and puffs up. Commercial coffee companies have touted puff-roasted coffee as yielding more cups per pounds and have used this as a rationale to sell the coffee at a higher price per pound.

This is not to say that the new technology is only for roasters concerned with extracting the least number of defects possible from a bad coffee. Specialty roasters who use the equipment to roast high-quality coffees have found that the new equipment will deliver an entirely different flavor profile than traditional equipment. The faster roasting tends to leave far more acidity in the cup than traditional roasters. It is therefore possible to have a dark-roasted coffee with a high level of acidity. It seems that the fast-roast technology may be weak in bringing out the maximum degree of aromatics that drum roasters can develop. (The fast roasters tend to suspend the coffee on a bed of hot, circulating air, or spin it in large bowl-like areas, unlike drum roasters, which roll the coffee in a rotating drum fitted with interior blades that keep the coffee turning over on itself.)

The flavor of a good-quality coffee will be muted by a quick roast. Conversely, a long roast will lead to a wheaty, "baked" flavor, which has neither the advantage of a dark roast nor the characteristics of a light roast. Again, roasting is a dynamic process of compromises: slow, even development versus baking; minimal exposure to the roasting process via heat and speed versus losing a lot of flavor with the same factors. Every coffee will respond differently.

People roasting fine-quality coffees in the United States have their own approaches to the enterprise. If one generalization can be made of those who are successful, it is that they have all developed highly personalized styles. This variety of styles yields very different end products from identical lots of green coffee. (See Section III, page 83, for interviews with coffee roasters that illustrate the stylistic variances of fine coffee.)

There is a great deal of controversy in the specialty-coffee community about what actually happens during the roasting process and which methods of roasting shed the most flattering light on particular coffees. Some roasters use the same process of roasting for all coffees, and the final color of the coffee bean is often the guiding light in determining when a roast is complete. Others not only roast different coffees to different degrees but vary the temperature over time in such complex and esoteric patterns, while varying the airflow through the roaster, that they give the impression of a modern-day Paganini pulling this lever, adjusting that valve and finally, in a climax of steam and smoke, allowing the crackling beans to pour out of the roaster in a crescendo of aromatic virtuosity. Still, one wonders if some roasters actually know what they're doing.

⚜ BLENDING ⚜

Coffee has become denatured over the years in an incremental process that has been a series of mostly well-intentioned steps—given the natural desire on the part of large commercial roasters to make "a little" more money. These roasters have found, for example, that "a little" robusta (see page 11) in their blends "mellows" the brew, according to consumer-preference studies. Given the sort of bad taste that robustas have, many of these roasters have then found it necessary to add a little pelletized chaff in an effort to attenuate the grassy edge these blends take on.

(Chaff is the stuff that flakes off the green beans during roasting.) Adding chaff does take away the rather nasty flavor that robustas have, but in the long run the quality drops a notch. People have grown so accustomed to this low-quality coffee that their palates need to be reeducated to high-quality coffee. This reeducation has fallen to the smaller roaster, who, by virtue of his size, does not have the same concerns about profit margin that the large commercial roaster has. What, then, is the criteria for the proprietary blends you see in specialty coffee stores?

A lot has been written about how coffee ultimately should be blended. Guides generally start out by asserting that coffees are either light or heavy bodied. They then go on to suggest that blending light with heavy and ending up with medium is the best road to blending satisfaction. But this blending concept doesn't help much in developing a pleasing blend. Perhaps the reason for this is that blending is seen as an effort to make up for weaknesses rather than accentuating strengths, as in blending the body of Sumatran with the acidity of Guatemalan to arrive at a coffee with a bright taste and a full, but mild body. But it's possible to gain greater insight into the floweriness of a good Kenyan coffee when it is blended with a sweet Tres Rios Costa Rican coffee. Often the flavors present in a particular coffee can't be perceived in the presence of other, more concentrated attributes; it is for this reason that when coffee is professionally evaluated it is usually brewed, or cupped, very weak. Thus one coffee can be used to enhance another without contributing any profound traits of its own.

In commercial varieties, though, coffee is blended not for esthetics but economics. Weaknesses are crowded out by glaring defects that clamor for attention, while the skilled blender attempts to keep all the grating voices at the same pitch in order to produce the golden fleece of his trade: the consistent cup. This consistency of characteristically subdued defects becomes the identity of a given brand, and consumers—like city dwellers who can't sleep in silence—don't believe they're really drinking coffee when it isn't sour, hard, and harsh, not to mention being slightly fermented with a hint of iodine (a taste known to the trade as *hard*).

The small roaster blends to establish certain proprietary blends, which, if the ingredients are listed, are sold on the appeal of the coffees blended. If the ingredients of the blend are *not* strictly defined, the roaster is attempting to offer a particular taste, flavor, and aroma on a consistent basis. By necessity, this sort of blend will not always be composed of the same coffees, as lots will vary shipment to shipment and season to season. The large roaster also blends in order to offer the exact same coffee (and taste) to consumers year in and year out. It is impressive, if not tasteful, how consistent the products of the large commercial roasters are.

· *Blended versus Unblended* ·

Blending allows the roaster and the coffee drinker to exert a great deal of control over the final cup of coffee. If a particular style is desired, then blending is often the answer. But blending, by definition, is a compromise; for every gain there is usually a loss. In fine coffees a blend will never taste as clear and distinct as a good unblended coffee from a particular region, country, or farm. For a coffee to play solo, however, it must be very, very good.

The key to good blending is keeping in mind the vagaries of the coffee bean. This means recognizing that the availability and the taste of beans will differ due to natural and economic factors. Blending should be done by comparative samplings, not formulas. Coffees should be isolated into acidy, full bodied, and neutral. An acidic coffee should serve as the base of the blend, a full-bodied coffee should be added to achieve a good balance, and finally a neutral coffee can be added to counter acidity to the desirable point. Simple and consistent blends may also be achieved through a combination of darker- and lighter-roasted coffees. In the case of milder coffees this is especially successful.

Blending can issue entirely different results if it is undertaken before a roast as opposed to after. Neither process will result in an entirely even product—not that an even roast should necessarily be the goal. Blending before generally tends to smooth out the distinctions between different coffees, making for a more cohesive taste. Blending after allows the roaster to develop each type of coffee to its maximum potential, preserving the flavor characteristics of each coffee along the way. The decision is one of style and judgment. Economics plays a role, also, in that blending before is more convenient in terms of production. The smoother taste and the lower cost of blending before roasting make it the preferred method for larger roasters, but a small roaster may choose the same procedure for esthetic reasons.

II

HOW
TO BREW
the
PERFECT
CUP

A COFFEE REMEMBERS WHERE IT CAME FROM AND how it was raised: the soil, the weather, the processing, and the roasting all are recorded in the bean. Coffee in the cup is a short-lived snapshot of that history, and brewing is the developmental bath.

In photography, there is considerable latitude during the development process to interpret a particular shot one way or another, choosing which aspects to emphasize or underplay: you can bring out a particular area or obscure it; you can heighten the contrast or soften it. So, too, do brewing options offer different alternatives to interpreting the same roasted beans.

A perfect cup is attainable only if the coffee drinker is reconciled to a totally subjective interpretation. Coffee can be brewed as thin as tea or as thick as porridge—each is considered the perfect cup by their devotees. Through tasting we develop our subjective appreciation of coffee. Through brewing, we attempt to match the coffee at hand with our taste preferences.

✎ BREWING METHODS ✎

While the methods of brewing coffee are not as numerous as the kinds of coffee you can brew, there are still enough of them to confuse and delight us. Here are some of the more popular methods, along with a couple of more unusual ways, to extract a beverage from the bean. (This list was compiled with help from George Howell; see page 98.) Of course, everyone has his or her own favorite method, and as you have probably discovered about people involved with specialty coffee, everyone holds the staunch opinion that his or hers is the best.

The following descriptions are overviews of each method and the principles of brewing they represent. For a detailed how-to guide for each method, refer to the instructions that come with your particular maker.

❀ TURKISH This method was used throughout the Middle East and Greece. It is perhaps the original means of extracting liqueur from coffee beans. The process is simple and results in a very strong, sweet, and thick brew that I would find difficult to enjoy on a daily basis. As a ritual, the grinding of the coffee by hand in a special brass grinder is an enjoyable one after a Turkish or Middle Eastern meal. The coffee is ground, then placed in a pot, called an ibrit, with sugar and water and brought to a boil three times. It is served in small cups.

To judge your success with the Turkish method, ask yourself a few simple questions (and please excuse my cynicism):

1. Do you have to stir it with both hands?

2. Does it stay black when you pour milk into it?

3. When you stir it, does the spoon:

   a. Stand up by itself?

   b. Completely disintegrate?

❧ **PERCOLATOR** This method passes brewed coffee from a heated reservoir below up through the grounds above, again and again and again. Although accompanied by a comforting aroma and that distinct morning music as it gurgles away, the brew it produces is far from soothing. The familiar stainless steel pot, full of bubble and brew, is often seen in movies and TV serials of the fifties. Nostalgia aside, this is where I would like to keep it. There have also been recent reports that percolated coffee is correlated with high cholesterol.

❧ **DRIP** This is today's most popular method of brewing coffee, largely due to its convenience. Near-boiling water is poured slowly through the grounds, either manually through a cone containing a filter, or sprayed over the grounds by any of the numerous electric drip machines. Many electric models even come with timing devices so that morning zombies can clutch their first cup with little or no effort. It is important to remember that water temperature must be maintained at 195° F, so make sure you purchase a capable machine. Also, it is important to remove the pot from the "keep-warm" burner to prevent the coffee from deteriorating.

❧ **FRENCH PRESS** Often referred to as Melior, after a brand name of plunger pot, this method utilizes infusion and pressure. After placing ground coffee in the beaker, hot water is added to create a coffee "stew." This is allowed to steep, and then a plunger filter pushes the grounds to the bottom of the beaker, and the coffee is left at the top.

(*text continues on page 70*)

Vacuum

Percolator

French Press

Drip

French Drip

Espresso

Neapolitan Flip

The Filter Factor

Public awareness about environmental issues has shown tremendous growth in the past few years. One of the issues that has been hotly debated concerning coffee is the use of filters in drip-method brewing. Current options include the traditional white paper filters, an increasing variety of unbleached or "natural" paper filters, and "gold" filters made of steel mesh and overlaid with gold.

White filters bear the brunt of environmental and health concerns for consumers. These filters use chlorine to bleach the paper, which, when combined with naturally occurring lignin molecules in wood, may result in the formation of dioxins and furans. The Environmental Protection Agency (EPA) considers dioxin a carcinogen and, as with all carcinogens, considers there to be a risk at any level of exposure. The American Paper Institute (API) counters that there is so much dioxin present in the environment that it is inevitable that trace amounts will be found in anything tested. API has made comprehensive assessments that clearly demonstrate its products and the workplace are safe even when minute amounts of dioxin are found. In tests done by the FDA, no evidence of dioxins was found in coffee brewed using white filters, and the FDA does not consider them a risk. For an increasingly environmentally aware market however, there are larger issues at stake. Paper plants that bleach their products often pose environmental hazards, releasing the by-products of bleaching into nearby lakes and streams. In areas such as Wisconsin, Maine, and Louisiana, advisories have been posted prohibiting fishing in several rivers because of dioxins and warning against the dangers of eating contaminated fish.

The brown or "natural" filters, which don't utilize chlorine, or at least utilize it to a lesser extent, may make you feel more a friend of mother earth, but they too have their problems. Namely, they alter the coffee's taste. For the purpose of illustrating this, pour boiling water through a brown and a bleached white filter. The cup of water that tastes like cardboard and most likely has sediment floating in it is from the brown filter. And although you may brew coffee strong enough to hide this taste, it's detracting from the brew you're otherwise so careful about.

Furthermore, I'm not sure that the environmental impact of the brown filter is much better than its bleached counterpart, as a certain amount of pulp bleaching is necessary to obtain minimal performance characteristics in paper products, such as strength and absorbency.

If you are still set on using paper filters for your maker, there is a third option that recently became available. Oxygen-whitened paper filters utilize oxygen instead of chlorine in the initial bleaching process and chlorine dioxide in the later stages. Unlike chlorine, neither oxygen nor chlorine dioxide react to form dioxin or furan, thus eliminating the environmental and health concerns of using paper filters. The problem is that there seems to be no oxygen-bleaching manufacturing plant in the United States at this time. These filters are available through Green Mountain Filters, 33 Coffee Lane, Waterbury, Vermont 05676, who found a Canadian source for oxygen bleaching. This company is also a veritable gold mine of information concerning the dioxin debate.

I prefer the French press method of brewing, thereby avoiding the filter factor altogether. But don't think that you have to give up your drip method in order to attend the next Earth Day. Gold filters are an alternative to paper filters, albeit an initially expensive one. I argue that the gold filter, when the cost is amortized over its lifetime, becomes less expensive than paper because it is reusable for a number of years. Its long life also has the effect of creating less trash and saving trees at the same time. The gold filter has its own considerations: you must be careful about how you grind your coffee and you should be aware that like any other change in your brewing process the coffee will probably taste different. The brew colloids, the elements that give coffee its body and special texture in your mouth, pass unhindered through a gold filter because the metal does not trap any of the coffee's natural oils. I've had complaints from friends who find that their coffee becomes too strong. In this case I translate different as better.

The French press method produces coffee that allows more brewing substances (oils, colloids, etc.) to remain in the coffee than would be left by methods using paper filters. For this reason, many people of the "I like coffee I can chew" school consider this the perfect cup.

🌿 VACUUM   One of the showier and more unusual methods of brewing coffee. The problem here is that the equipment is not readily available.

As the water nears boiling it is forced up into a glass chamber with the coffee grounds. After all the water is in the upper chamber the mixture is allowed to steep and then the heat is turned off. As the temperature cools the coffee is sucked back down to the lower chamber by the vacuum. You then separate the two pots and serve. This makes for a fascinating (and quite loud) after-dinner entertainment and beverage in one.

ESPRESSO Stove-top versions, heated by the stove's burner, contain two chambers: water is in the bottom chamber and is forced up through a filter containing the coffee grounds. It arrives gurgling in the upper chamber and is served. There are also numerous electric countertop models which inject hot water through the coffee grounds directly into a cup, very much like those huge machines seen in coffeehouses. These home espresso machines have become almost as commonplace in the average kitchen as percolators were in those fifties movies I mentioned. Most models come with the means of steaming milk for cappuccinos and lattes.

COLD-WATER METHOD This method is not recommended for the impatient coffee drinker, although it is an especially useful means of making coffee for use in cold coffee drinks, recipes, and homemade liqueurs. Mix ground coffee with cold water in a large container (1 pound finely ground coffee to 1 quart cold water) and let set at room temperature for approximately 10 to 12 hours. This will create a coffee "extract." Strain out the grounds and refrigerate the extract and, when ready, fill a cup one fourth (or less) full. Fill the remainder of the cup with hot water, and drink up! There are a number of cold-water coffee makers on the market. There is evidence that using this method provides coffee that is easier on the stomach because it extracts fewer of the coffee's natural oils, making the coffee less acidic. This essence will keep refrigerated for weeks.

NEAPOLITAN FLIP This isn't the latest move in gymnastics, but an Italian twist on coffee making, also known as a reversible drip pot. The mechanism, usually made of aluminum, consists of two chambers, with coffee secured in between them. The lower chamber is filled with water, and the whole contraption is put on the stove. When the water is boiling, steam escapes from a pinhole below the coffee grounds. At this point the pot is removed from the stove and flipped over. Water drips through the grounds into the now right-side-up serving pot.

PRE-BREWING CARE AND CONSIDERATIONS

• Handling Your Beans •

Coffee's short-lived nature is a clue to its proper handling. It should be roasted, ground, brewed, and consumed quickly to avoid deterioration. While complex, coffee is best understood as a flash of flavor and aroma; the sorting-out of its tastes and aromas—the connoisseurship—comes after. Coffee is, after all, perishable. It begins to go stale as soon as it has been roasted, and within weeks roasted beans will lose their flavor. Espresso and dark roasts last somewhat longer, but this is probably because their strong taste tends to cover any staleness. Grinding accelerates the staling process, causing coffee to lose its flavor within hours, not only because the integrity of the bean is broken down but because more surface area of the bean is exposed to air, the number-one staling agent. Because of the volatile nature of coffee's flavor, special care should be taken when storing it.

The most significant cause of flavor loss is exposure to air, which causes the oils responsible for coffee's aroma and flavor to evaporate. For this reason, coffee should always be stored in an airtight container. The loss of flavor and aroma due to air exposure is clearly demonstrated when you open a can of commercial coffee and get that first wonderfully aromatic whiff. Most of the coffee's essential oils are contained in that air you just released, meaning it's not in the coffee where it belongs. This also explains why the aroma is not as obvious in subsequent openings of the same can. Instant coffees actually have coffee aroma sprayed into them to get that same aromatic effect. Many people recommend storing coffee in the refrigerator once it is ground in order to maintain freshness. However, just as many claim that this is a bad idea because moisture will inevitably condense on the grounds each time the container is opened, thereby speeding the staling process. After air, water is the second biggest threat to coffee freshness. The best solution to this argument is to invest in a grinder, and grind only as much coffee as you need at a time. Keep your beans in an airtight container on the counter or in your cupboard. If long-range storage is a necessity, it is best to freeze the beans in moisture-proof containers, and simply remove and grind what you need for immediate use. No need to thaw. The beans will keep the majority of their flavor for up to three months if they are carefully packed and kept frozen.

You should also remember that coffee picks up odors from other foods, and so you should be wary of the wrong neighbors. If it is stored next to strong-smelling foods such as onions, garlic, etc., you'll wind up with an interesting twist on your normal brew, and probably not a desirable one either.

• *The Daily Grind* •

One of the worst things to do to your coffee is to speed up its already brief shelf life. And yet, that's what most people unknowingly do. I'll admit that the temptation is great to have your coffee ground at the store. After all, time is of the essence in the modern household, but, to render the perfect cup, there is no substitution for freshly ground coffee. (If you must have your coffee ground

10 Keys to Perfect Coffee

While there may be several important steps to brewing your personal perfect cup, there are essential things one should always remember, regardless of the method used.

1. Make sure that your equipment is cleaned thoroughly and often. Dirty equipment can add strange tastes to your coffee.
2. Quality, quality, quality. If you don't start out with great beans you can never make great coffee.
3. The same as above but apply it to the water you are using (see page 75).
4. Grind the coffee just before brewing (see page 76).
5. Make sure you're using the correct grind for your method (see page 76).
6. Use the right amount of ground coffee—two tablespoons per six-ounce cup. Too many

for you, have it done in small enough amounts that you use it quickly, and store the ground coffee in an airtight container.)

An important consideration when you do grind your coffee is the variation in grinds. This has to do with the method of brewing, or more specifically with the degree of extraction, which indicates the amount of flavor removed from the grounds. This might sound complicated, but it is only simple logic. The degree of extraction depends on two things: the fineness of the grind, and the length of contact the grounds have with water, coarsely people wind up with weak coffee because the right amount seems too much.

7. A trade secret: fill your mug with hot water to warm it up before you pour your coffee in. This keeps the coffee hot longer.

8. Before serving the coffee, stir it. The amount of extraction tends to change over time when you are using certain methods. By giving it a quick stir you guarantee that the flavor is consistent throughout the pot.

9. If you're making more than you can drink at one sitting, store the coffee in a thermos and not on the burner. Staying on the burner will give the coffee a burnt, bitter taste.

10. If you've gone to all this trouble, take the time to make your cup of coffee count. Don't gulp, savor.

ground coffee requiring longer contact with water. This means that for quick methods, such as espresso, the grind should be very fine. For slower methods such as drip, the grind should be medium.

• *You're Only As Good As Your Water* •

So you've gotten yourself a great coffee, roasted to perfection. You've stored it correctly, you ground it thirty seconds ago, and you're ready to make the perfect cup of

The Basics of Good Grinding

The grinds required for various brewing methods and the approximate time required for that grind using a simple electric hand grinder are as follows:

Cold-water method/percolator: Coarse grind; 5 to 10 seconds

Electric/drip method/French press: Medium grind; 10 seconds

Vacuum method/Neapolitan flip: Fine grind; 15 seconds

Filter-cone drip method/espresso machines: Very fine grind; 30 seconds

In order to ensure an even grind it is best to shake a hand grinder gently while using it, otherwise the grind will be finer on the bottom and coarser at the top. If you wind up with an uneven grind, the extraction will differ, and ultimately the brew will suffer.

coffee. But wait! One of the easiest things to forget is that coffee has another ingredient. In fact, that other ingredient—water—makes up 98 to 99 percent of the beverage. This doesn't sound like it should require much thought, just the turning of the wrist required to turn the handle on your kitchen faucet. There are a couple of important considerations, however. When making coffee, the water should be cold (and don't forget to let it run for a few seconds to allow it to aerate before filling your pot or kettle). For the best possible brew, the water should be free of any flavor or odor taints. This simple requirement however, disqualifies water from over 90 percent of the United States. (I believe that our water in Los Angeles actually glows in the dark. Which, naturally, disqualifies it from being used in coffee.) For the serious coffee drinker then, it is best to either invest in a filtering system or to have a water delivery service.

⋙ ESPRESSO YOURSELF ⋘

One of the most confused terms in coffee is *espresso*. Espresso is a method of brewing and not, as many people mistakenly assume, a type of bean or a degree of roast, although it commonly refers to both. Espresso, the brewing

(*text continues on page 80*)

Making Espresso at Home

For most coffee fanatics the home espresso-cappuccino machine has become a *must*. There is only one small problem, and that is learning how to make the same sensual-looking drink that your smiling and confident *barista* serves you, instead of a mess of grounds and limp foam. Here are some of the basics of home espresso making that we've managed to get out of our favorite *baristas*.

1. As long as the coffee is very finely ground, espresso can be made from any kind of coffee roasted in any style. My favorite is a blend of Kenya AA, Costa Rican, or Guatemalan, and Sumatra Mandheling, medium roast.

2. Be sure to pack the grounds—approximately 7 grams (2 tsp.) to 2 ounces (4 tbsp.) of water—carefully. If they're too tightly packed, the water can't get through, the espresso will taste burnt, and you will end up with dry spots in your *gruppa* (the metal cup that holds the grounds). If they're packed too light, you will get a watered-down version, without the concentrated body and flavor a true espresso should have. There is no way to describe how to pack grounds perfectly. It will take practice. Examine your gruppa to see how you're doing, then readjust your packing. It is best to start with a few gentle taps of the packer that comes with the machine.

3. Having applied the perfect amount of pressure to your grounds, fill the appropriate chamber

with water and put the metal filter cup in place (into the bottom chamber if you're using a stovetop machine, or into the metal holder if you're using a countertop machine). Turn on your machine and out will come steaming black liquid. If you're successful there will be a creamy beige layer floating on top of the coffee called the *crema*. If you're making cappuccino, now comes the challenging part.

4. There are two schools of thought when it comes to steaming milk: start with either lukewarm milk or ice-cold milk. I suggest you try both and find out which is most successful for you. The lukewarm school insists that the pitcher and the milk should be room temperature; the ice-cold school insists on adding ice and keeping the pitcher of milk refrigerated. Either way the method is as follows: make sure that the machine is up to full steam; place the nozzle in the milk, keeping it barely immersed at the top edge of the milk; and as the foam builds up, keep the nozzle moving up with it.

5. Ignore everything we've just said and practice making the perfect cappuccino alone in the privacy of your own kitchen for at least two weeks straight. Or put in a job application at your favorite coffee retailer.

Mr. Espresso

When I decided I needed to know about espresso, I called the man who takes his company name from the beverage, Carlo Di Ruocco, the owner of Mr. Espresso Company in Alameda, California. Carlo was born in Salerno, Italy. He grew up and trained as a coffee-roasting apprentice to a man in Naples who was kind enough to share with him a tremendous love for coffee and the art of roasting. A conversation with Carlo will quickly convince you of the merits of the beloved beverage. Here's the origin of espresso, in Carlo's words:

"It is said in Italy that an impatient gentleman from Naples asked an engineer from Milano to speed up the process of brewing coffee because his primitive Neapolitan coffeepot took too long. As a result, Mr. Bezzera patented the first espresso machine in 1903, capable of delivering a lightly concentrated beverage with strong flavor and aroma—also known as *espresso*.

"This application of a little Italian imagination resulted in boosting the sale of Italian products all over the world, for, until then, the only exports were Ferraris.

"During my many years' experience in the espresso industry I have heard many different explanations for the origin of the term *espresso,* such as *quick, fast, instant,* etc. The real definition of *espresso* is 'a beverage which is made at the moment it is requested.'

---

method (see page 73), refers to a quick infusion of water through coffee grounds using either a stovetop or countertop machine.

Through common misuse, however, espresso has also become a term synonymous with dark-roasted coffee. As

"This is different from filtered coffee, which usually is produced in multiple servings in advance. Therefore, while the quality of filtered coffee depends on the time elapsed from preparation to consumption, the time factor has no effect on espresso.

"The difference between the two methods is obvious. The beverages produced are different both from a chemical-physical and an organoleptic standpoint. (Organoleptic examination is how foods are evaluated. It simply means employing one or more of your sensory organs. With coffee you employ all of them, except perhaps your ears.) Filter coffee is a clear liquid that contains a very small quantity of solid material, while espresso, being a multiphase system, (solids suspended in liquid, oils in colloidal suspension, and dissolved solids), contains small quantities of solid particles in suspension.

"From the organoleptic point of view, as compared to filtered coffee, espresso has much more body, a more pleasant aftertaste, and a richer flavor and aroma. Drinking espresso involves not only taste and smell, as in the case of filtered coffee, but also appearance. A good espresso should have a thick, long-lasting cream, *la crema del caffè*" (see page 79 for a discussion of espresso's "cream").

such, "espresso roast" may be used to refer to coffee roasted on the dark side or blended by a particular merchant for use in making espresso. This increases the chances for total confusion, causing some people to think that they are buying beans grown in Italy. Well, the climate in Italy isn't hospitable to coffee trees, and the truth is that espresso, the roast, may be made from any bean, roasted any style from light to dark.

Although there seems to be a profusion of "espresso bars" throughout the country, most of the people in them are not drinking espresso, but espresso drinks cut with milk, such as cappuccino and caffé latte. As with most things Italian there is a certain aura of romance about these drinks. Anyone who's experienced the dense, aromatic, and somehow sweet flavor of espresso, or has had the pleasure of tickling an upper lip with the creamy foam of cappuccino knows why. And it seems that having had that pleasure, more and more people are attempting to reproduce it in their own kitchen.

III

HOW
TO BUY
COFFEE
and
WHOM TO
BUY IT FROM

O F THIS BOOK'S MANY PREMISES, ONE IS
pivotal: that the regional specialty-coffee
roaster shares much in common with the small quality-
conscious winemaker. First of all, each depends a great
deal on his or her own interpretation of an agricultural
product. Second, the consistency of that interpretation is
almost as important as its quality.

· *Interpreting an Agricultural Product* ·

In the consumption of a commodity that has been interpreted by a craftsman (the chef, the wine maker, the coffee
roaster), we taste not only the particular end product (pâté,
Rioja, Mocha-Java) but also the qualities of the land that it
came from: the smell of the wind, the feel of the soil, the
particular light and warmth of the sun, even the fragrance
of the surrounding vegetation.

The taste of a hard, tannic Bordeaux feels somehow hotter than a damp, musty Burgundy. A rough-textured "country pâté" might remind us of a day's visit to a back-road farm. And if a cup of coffee simply tastes good, it's not as great as one that reminds you it came from a *place* and that *people* grew it, people who pulled each cherry from the tree with their work-hardened hands.

We know that coffees from different parts of the world taste different from one another (see chart on page 38). Coffees from different farms in the same area do, too. Each describes a place and a history. The taste of a coffee has a lot to say about which nutrients were incorporated into it; the phrase *goût de terroir,* ("tang of the soil") used to explain the distinctive local tastes of wine, can also refer to coffee.

If enough care has been given to the development of a coffee it will have lots to give back in the cup. Some coffees bring with them the smells of the forests they grew near, the taste of the water that soaked their roots, the flavors of the fruits that grew near them. There is an aged Indian coffee called Monsoon Malabar that exudes an aroma of turmeric and cardamom, and one whiff puts you in a Bombay bazaar. Philippine robustas taste like the rubber trees near which they are grown. (In fact, this coffee feels rubbery, too, covering the tongue with a palpable latex coat.)

• *Coffee Roasting as an Art?* •

Coffee is a raw material that, like wine grapes, is capable of an extraordinary transformation into a unique beverage. The roaster then is not just a person who turns on a piece of machinery, but someone who sees green coffee as a medium that has the ability to create a sensual impact. Much like visual artists, creative roasters can use the same medium and end up with completely different results. And, as

Beans Emptying from
a Roaster

in the visual arts, the beauty in coffee is to a certain extent a matter of personal taste.

• *The Consistency of the Roaster's Interpretation* •

There are a lot of wine makers, chefs, and coffee roasters who are very good at what they do. Some produce interpretations of their products that are, more often than not, brilliant. But before these craftsmen can be considered artists, their efforts have to be able to be repeated again and again; then it can be said that they have developed a style. However your retailer-roaster decides to interpret the perfect coffee, the coffees should maintain enough consistency in their blending and roasting so that you can depend on the appearance, flavor, and experience of the coffee you buy week after week. Although subtle variations are inevitable, given the variable nature of coffee itself, it quickly becomes frustrating to have your favorite Sumatra taste different week to week.

 ## CHOOSING A ROASTER-RETAILER

Perhaps the most important factor in choosing a specialty-coffee retailer is learning what you like. As you will see from the following profiles we've accumulated of roasters and retailers throughout the country, each one has his or her own opinion, and generally a strong one, about what makes the perfect cup. The retailer you choose should have an inventory that meets your tastes and demands, and he or she should provide a consistent level of quality.

It may take some time before you can determine what your tastes are, or perhaps you have already established your criteria. Whatever your level of coffee sophistication, you should shop for a coffee retailer just as you would for a baker or wine merchant to provide your everyday bread and table wine.

Some important questions you should ask yourself when selecting a retailer are:

1. Does the retailer have a consistent approach to roasting and blending?

2. Are the coffees fresh?

3. Do the beans of each coffee type and blend consistently look the same?

4. Does my retailer have forthright answers on the various decaf processes and which type of coffees are available?

You should also feel confident that your retailer is properly labeling and representing the coffees you are buying. This means that when you pay a premium for an expensive coffee such as Kona or Celebes (Sulawesi), you're sure of what you are getting. You should be able to distinguish different tastes from general type to general type: Ethiopian shouldn't taste like Costa Rican.

Given the volatile nature of coffee prices, your retailer should also be in touch with the coffee market in order to provide you with up-to-date, easy-to-understand information when price changes occur. In order for you to be able to assess your retailer, you should be able to speak the language and have a basic understanding of these issues.

Your relationship with the retailer's staff is also an important consideration. You must have confidence in their ability to meet your needs. For this reason it's important to ask as many questions as possible. Do they understand the differences in decafs? Can they lead you towards a high-acidity coffee? Does their idea of a full-city roast and yours correspond? Once you have had some of the basic questions answered, it will help you determine which supplier to choose.

Profiles in Coffee:
• A Sampling of America's Best Coffee Purveyors •

The proliferation of specialty coffee retailers and roasters over the last twenty years is astounding. In many areas of the country there are specialty-coffee shops on every corner or in every mall. Of the thousands of retailers specializing in quality coffee, there must be many hundreds that meet the standards I've identified above. Below are interviews with just a fraction of America's fine coffee people. My goal in giving you these profiles is to introduce you to some dedicated, honest-to-goodness coffee roaster-retailers who share one thing in common: dedication to providing you with the best coffee. So read through the profiles and use them to familiarize yourself with some of the prevailing attitudes, and prepare yourself for a lot of conflicting opinions. Then, armed with your own attitudes and opinions, you can feel confident about what you buy and whom you buy it from.

GILLIES COFFEE COMPANY
New York, New York

During the financial panic of 1837, Wright Gillies left the family homestead in Newburgh-on-Hudson to seek his fortune in the big city. He worked hard and took pride in his work. In 1840 he successfully struck out on his own in the coffee business, roasting his beans in the courtyard behind his Washington Street shop. This humble beginning in backyard roasting allows Gillies to proclaim itself the oldest coffee merchant in America, having been in business for over 150 years. Today Don Shoenholt, his partner Hy Chabbot, and their crew continue to follow the traditions of the original Mr. Gillies with the loving attention that coffee, this special gift of nature, deserves from the hand of man.

Donald M. Schoenholt, chief executive of Gillies, has been with the family enterprise since 1963, but only because his dad wouldn't let him into the business at an earlier age than seventeen. Legend has it that David L.

Schoenholt used to change and burp Donald between roasts. Cupping-table games revolving around the tastes of various varietals were everyday fare at the Schoenholt home. "While this was going on," Donald recalls, "my grandmother would worry that coffee would stunt my growth." The skills he learned at his father's knee helped pay for many a lunch during Don's teenage years, as he could always win a bet by guessing the brand of coffee being served at the coffee shop or cafeteria where he and his friends ate lunch.

Today, Don's cupping skills have passed into Gillies folklore, along with his well-deserved reputation as a champion of uncompromised coffee. Don still personally supervises every roast of Gillies coffee. His belief in hands-on management is a reflection of his understanding of the coffee business as a personal relationship between Gillies and the people they serve. Don's love of coffee is also evident in his role as spokesman for the coffee trade, through his many articles and his participation in the founding of the Specialty Coffee Association of America, the Specialty Coffee Taskforce of the Coffee Brewing Center, and the Coffee Kids Foster Parents Plan.

Gillies, with less than twenty employees, prides itself on being a small, quality-based company. The New York market is small geographically, but crowded with upscale retailers and restaurateurs. In this competitive market Gillies has earned and maintained a respected position.

Concerning flavored coffee, an area of some heated debate within the specialty-coffee trade, Don comments, "There are many in the trade who view flavored coffee as 'unclean.' This is an unfortunate and uneducated view as it does not incorporate an understanding of coffee's history. Flavoring coffee is as old as the beverage itself. Abyssinian tribesmen added cloves and Arabian merchants cardamom to their favorite beverage centuries ago. Cream and sugar have been a tradition of coffee flavoring in Western society since coffee's first introduction." While he doesn't care for the idea of nachos-flavored coffee, he believes that to deny the facts of history and the wants of the public is an error.

Donald's personal coffee changes with the seasons and the arrival of new varietals, but his method is invariably a European automatic-drip system, utilizing a gold-impregnated mesh filter. At home, however, it's another story. The Schoenholts continue to serve Mocha & Java Style, the coffee Mom always served.

The philosophy of Gillies is that their coffees should reflect their spirit, their bias for the best, and their temperament and intellect. This fixation with excellence is reflected in the many honors and accolades Gillies has received through the years.

ZABAR'S
New York, New York

Most people are aware that Zabar's has become an institution over the past twenty years, a one-stop shop for almost anything delectable. Zabar's was founded in the thirties and had expanded to a five-store chain by the late 1950s. At that time they had an extensive grocery selection, kept late hours, and were open seven days a week.

During the sixties Zabar's trimmed down to one store specializing in great food at reasonable prices. They started closing earlier (except for Saturday until midnight). At that time, Saul Zabar, one of the founder's three sons, took over the supervision of the coffee and the smoked fish as part of his responsibilities. Saul started personally roasting all of his coffee in Brooklyn around this time and has been doing it ever since.

Fine coffee has always been part of Zabar's tradition. Fifteen years ago, before becoming involved in the coffee business, I went to Zabar's for the first time to try the coffee. It tasted good but was different than what I was used to on the West Coast. Aside from the sheer volume (twelve to fifteen thousand pounds a week) of coffee that Zabar's sells, and their relative prominence in the minds of many coffee aficionados, it is that difference that prompts me to include them here.

Saul Zabar roasts his coffee light. He thinks of coffee like fine wine, and he wants acidity in all the coffee he sells. Many roasters will talk about the point in roasting coffee at which you start to lose acidity and gain body and aromatics. That "razor's edge," as Saul Zabar thinks of it, is what coffee roasting is all about. Because this approach yields such a different taste and character than what most roasters sell, people often wonder if he isn't using radically different coffees. He is not. Zabar's does not offer fancy-name estate coffees, as some roasters do, but carefully selects strictly hard beans for their acidic character. The difference all comes down to roast color, and people either love it or they don't.

Another area of controversy for Zabar's has been the subject of Jamaican Blue Mountain coffee. Zabar's exclusive East Coast ties to the Jamaican coffee board extended for over two decades. During that time, however, investment from other countries and a general erosion in the consistency and quality of Jamaican coffee have created a situation in which genuine Jamaican Blue Mountain coffee, while more readily available, is not worth the price. Zabar's, therefore, sells a blend they call Blue Mountain Style, which they feel approximates the qualities one used to find in the genuine article but at a substantially lower price. This coffee contains no beans from Jamaica.

Generally, the goal of Zabar's with regard to coffee is to consistently deliver what Saul believes is the best-tasting coffee at a reasonable price. This is the general policy throughout Zabar's.

You would expect one of the partners of one of the best specialty-food stores in the country to look, if not plump, at least very well fed. Saul Zabar is no candidate for starvation, but he is a very slender fellow, and while he clearly enjoys the stuff he nibbles on as he walks through Zabar's, it is equally clear that his enjoyment is in the flavor, taste, and aroma of the food, not in the consumption. In the factory where he roasts his coffee we spent several hours cupping together. Saul washes his own glasses, grinds his own samples, and takes calls on a single-line phone with no answering machine. While cupping, Saul will point out the razor's edge in roasting that allows for acidity and flavor. Achieving his goal, considering the volume involved, can be tormenting. He tastes and evaluates all his roasts and makes notes, and is constantly adjusting a little darker or a little lighter. He has a perfectionist nature. And if, like Saul, you like your coffee brisk and flavorful like a young wine, you will never be disappointed. He knows exactly what he wants to deliver, and he delivers it.

OREN'S DAILY ROAST
New York, New York

Oren Bloostein is one of the newer names in the coffee business. His interest in specialty coffee came in a roundabout way. "I was working at Saks Fifth Avenue as an assistant buyer, and living in an apartment house that had a coffee store in it. I liked retailing, but didn't like what I was doing exactly. This guy who owned the coffee store looked like he had a great life. Only open eight hours a day, five days a week, four in the summer." After investigating the expenses of opening a store in New York, and finding out the cost of roasted coffee, the idea of a relaxing work week turned into something very different. "I figured it would be me behind the counter, in a dilapidated building, hoping they didn't tear my store down." Oren finally quit Saks, and went to business school. His interest in coffee hadn't left, and while doing a marketing paper on the subject he saw an ad for a roasting machine. "A little light bulb went on. All of a sudden everything looked not only possible, but better than I had imagined it." Oren dropped his studies and looked for store space.

Open since 1985, Oren's Daily Roast currently has two stores and a roasting factory, with plans for opening a third location this year. "We used to roast in the back of the original store, but it became physically impossible to roast enough coffee." The importance of keeping up with fresh roasting is simple. "Since we roast the coffee ourselves, we can offer more coffee, better coffee, and lower prices." This philosophy is what has made Oren's a success, but the demise of coffee in most of today's market has also helped. "We're fortunate where we are because there is a relatively good awareness of coffee. Manhattan is full of delis and markets with plastic containers full of coffee. The problem is that most of it is stale and horrible. People are used to buying coffee in this manner; they come to me, and the same thing fresh is a pleasant change. Once they buy fresh, they're hooked."

There's more to his roasting than the frequency: there is an approach that is entirely individual. "I roast to the way I like it. It's not as dark as some roasts, but definitely a lot darker than what you generally see in New York. I think you get more flavor from the darker roast. We roast to what I think the peak of flavor is. We don't roast to achieve a certain percentage of shrinkage; we roast it until it's ready." To keep coffee as fresh as possible the roasting is done in small batches, then shipped regularly to the stores. Another important and elemental aspect of Oren's success is honesty. "We label everything; there are no secrets. Almost everything is sold straight." The blends that Oren does sell are labeled with the varieties used, and if someone wants the recipe, he'll be glad to provide it. "I'm not worried about someone else being able to duplicate my products, because it can't be done. You can't find the quality and freshness elsewhere."

Like many people in the business, Oren has a hard time selecting his own favorite coffee. "One that I drink more often is Celebes Kalossi. A sensational coffee. I love the full body, the smooth, syrupy spicy flavor." His love of coffee depends heavily on one crucial element: quality. The method is a secondary consideration, although he most often brews up his perfect cup using a Chemex cone. "One thing I've learned, even in the short time I've been in the business, is that you can taste quality in the coffee." This is what he hopes to pass on to his clientele: "Buy better beans."

In discussing the more debatable topics of specialty coffee, Oren admitted to an openness that comes from being the new kid on the block. "I have very few preconceived ideas about coffee. However, I may not be as unbiased about things after I've been in the business for ten years." His stores carry both Swiss-water- and European-water-processed decafs. "People are very concerned, and many of my customers only want water process. Other people are willing to trust me enough to believe I carry methylene chloride because it's safe and has a better flavor." Daily Roast also sells their own flavored coffees. "They're a big seller, but I hate flavoring the coffee. I don't like touching it at all. I don't like my hands to smell like chocolate mint for three days."

For Oren, the most appealing thing about being involved with specialty coffee is the satisfaction of doing something well. "I enjoy retailing *our* coffee. Prices are not as cheap as I originally wanted them to be, but then I found out how good our coffee was in comparison to what people were used to. Working in coffee is terrific because people walk into my store and smile. No matter what kind of a day they're having, they smell the coffee and they smile. People really appreciate the effort that goes into making the product the best. Even the people who don't understand the process appreciate it in the cup."

BUCKS COUNTY COFFEE ROASTING
Langhorne, Pennsylvania

Eight years ago, Rodger Owen's business was nuts, quite literally: colossal cashews, mammoth pecans, and giant macadamias. He soon found out, however, that having nothing in his store but nuts made for a lot of shelf space. Searching for a quality product to help fill the empty space, he bought seventy-five pounds of coffee beans and began experimenting. Today Bucks County Coffee Company roasts about seven hundred pounds of coffee daily and has fifteen stores, all with packed shelves. Rodger also owns and operates The Squire's Choice, a national mail-order business featuring freshly roasted coffee and nuts, as well as specialty candy and popcorn.

The philosophy that enabled Rodger to make the transition from cashews to Kona was his emphasis on learning every element of the business. "I know how to buy it, how to roast it, and how to sell it," he says. For the subtler nuances of the coffee business, which the process of cupping demands, Rodger chooses to rely on the expertise of others. "I don't have the taste for coffee that many other people in the business do. My opinion remains objective. I know that we're good because our customers keep coming back."

The main reasons customers are coming back may be that Rodger is a customer-oriented businessman, fastidious about quality. "We don't buy our beans on price. We buy the best, not the cheapest. We work hard, from 7 a.m.

to 10 p.m." This dedication is evident in the roasting at Bucks County. Roasting is viewed as an art, with special attention to each batch and individual type of coffee. According to Rodger, Bucks County Coffee Roasting Company's objective is to make the best possible coffee.

Concerning flavored coffees, Rodger believes the same principle applies to coffee and alcoholic beverages. "People begin their consumption with something sweet. As people try flavored coffees, they get interested in coffee as a whole, and begin drinking nonflavored specialty coffee."

With locations as varied as a Farmer's Market in Ardmore, Pennsylvania, and a high-profile coffee bar and bakery at Union Station, Washington, D.C., Rodger has noticed that local preferences revolve around espresso and flavored coffees. He has also discovered that although anyone can afford a cup of coffee, their clientele is upscale. However, in Rodger's opinion, more young people are entering the consumer market.

It is the customer who motivates Rodger, and keeps him interested in the business. "Coffee is a product which is consumed every day; therefore, it has the possibility of reaching a wide spectrum of consumers. There is a theory that the United States is losing its work ethic and its interest in quality. Specialty coffee is a field where this philosophy doesn't hold. I like working with consumers who take such an interest in quality."

COFFEE CONNECTION
Brighton, Massachusetts

George Howell grew up in Mexico City, went to school in places like Berkeley, California, and settled in Boston before opening the Coffee Connection in 1975. There are now nine Coffee Connections in the Boston area.

When I first met George he picked me up at Logan Airport and took me to his store near Harvard Square, which is in a refurbished parking garage. The first thing I noticed were the Huichol yarn paintings on the walls. George had originally come to Boston, in fact, to exhibit these paintings and other artworks, but "economic need and coffee deprivation" created the impetus for him to found the Coffee Connection. Having been exposed to specialty coffee on the West Coast, and already beginning to question the roasts and selections of what he had been drinking, establishing the Coffee Connection was a personal quest as well as a business venture.

The Huichol Indians live a two-days' walk from the nearest roads in central Mexico. Although there has been much written on the Huichol, most of it distorted and sensationalized, no one, in my opinion, has been able to define or capture the subtle mysticism and complexity of their culture, much less their art as manifested in the yarn paintings.

George approaches coffee the same way that the shaman artists of the Huichol express their view of reality through their complex, wildly colorful, yet restrained yarn paintings. As far as George is concerned, the questions are never answered, and the essence of each of the coffees he sells is never completely established, just as the yarn paintings raise new questions each time you see them.

More than perhaps any other roaster in the country, the Coffee Connection focuses on selling the most quintessential example from each coffee-producing country. If there is a particular estate in a given country where the farmer is doing everything he can to produce the best coffee he can, George, if he knows about it, will buy it. This doesn't necessarily mean that George Howell sells the "best" coffee. There are several roasters who feel that too much attention during growing, harvesting, and processing can strip a coffee of much of its charm (in addition to adding to its price), but that isn't the point of George's efforts. He's trying to purify and identify the core essence of each origin: what is it that makes Guatemalan Antigua so good? Is it the smokiness? Which roast brings it out the most? And so it goes with every coffee that George sells.

George and his roastmaster, Robert Dattala, will cup and recup their coffees, constantly adjusting the roast with every sampling. Each time a new sample comes in they will compare it to what they have, always trying to make sure that they have what they feel they can define as the best.

Right now, the "best" includes Costa Rica La Minita, San Miguel Genuine Antigua, Haanio Estate Kona, rare estate Kenya AA+'s, and a Mandheling that is unique in its clean, crisp flavor.

The Coffee Connection, like other roasters in the United States who share a dedication to quality, spends a great deal of time making an effort to keep employees informed not only about the coffees sold but also about brewing methods and the vagaries of each lot of coffee that comes in. In addition, the Coffee Connection is the only specialty retailer I know of that prints the day of the roast on each bag of coffee sold.

J. MARTINEZ & CO. COFFEE MERCHANTS
Atlanta, Georgia

John Martinez represents the fourth generation of his family to have been involved in the coffee business. At one time his family even grew their own coffee on their own plantation in Jamaica. From John's father to his great-grandfather, the Martinez family has been involved in coffee, and his college-age son is currently in the process of becoming fully apprenticed. When asked how specialty coffee crossed into his personal life, John answered, "Coffee *is* my life; I am always talking about it."

Over the past couple of years John has seen two major trends evolving in the specialty-coffee industry. America in the past five to ten years has learned how to recognize and procure quality coffee. "Americans have been fed bad coffee on good advertising for years," John explains. "In the gourmet trade, it is the opposite relationship. It is very easy to tell the difference between good, fresh, properly roasted coffee and commercial coffee, so the gourmet trade does not rely on heavy advertising."

Secondly, there is an emerging trend towards good decaffeinated coffee. In the controversy over chemically decaffeinated coffee, John agrees that "chemical tastes better." But, as John exclaimed, there is nowhere he can find decaffeinated coffee that meets his standards. About the new CO_2 process, he says, "One day you can have a beautiful test, and the next is unremarkable. Once they achieve consistent results, I see CO_2 as the replacement for chemical decaffeination." To avoid all these problems, John ships his own green coffee to a company in Switzerland to be decaffeinated. "I know the pedigree of my coffee is impeccable, and there are very few brokers who themselves know what they're buying." One of the trends I brought up was the movement towards organic foods. In the production of coffee, John sees this as a fad. "A coffee plantation takes as long as ten years to be brought to a point where it is producing, and it can be wiped out by an overseas fungus or bug infestation in no time. For this reason, I don't see organic coffee as a lasting trend."

At J. Martinez & Co., none of the coffees are blended. Martinez believes that good coffee stands on its own. This avoids the problem of mislabeling, which is often responsible for disappointing coffee drinkers. People may pay for Jamaican Blue Mountain or Kona and simply be getting a blend that contains some of this coffee. John feels strongly that if people are going to blend they should label the contents of their coffee.

Roasting at J. Martinez is part of an ongoing educational process. Teaching people what good roasting tastes like is looked on as something akin to spreading the gospel. It is John's opinion that most of the specialty roasters in America over-roast coffee. The strength of his conviction is conveyed by his story, "If I were king of Coffee Land these people [the over-roasters] would be punished. They would be forced to pick the bugs off the trees on the organic farms." The confidence John feels in his own roasting technique shows in the unconditional guarantee he provides with his coffees. Its success is demonstrated by the fact that he has had only one return in the year he has been in business. "A customer got a medium-roast coffee, and felt the coffee was flat. He was used to burnt coffee, and so I sent him dark roast." Roasting is done in small quantities. Using a Probat thirty-kilo roaster, coffee is roasted fifteen pounds at a time. "The maximum amount that should be roasted when you are doing gourmet coffee is fifty pounds. My development plan will not be a bigger roaster; it will be to get two roasters."

Concerning flavored coffees, he says, "I cannot flavor coffee because I cannot taint my warehouse. The green coffee picks up the flavoring." John does, however, provide flavoring that his customers may take home and add to their coffee beans. The sensitivity of beans to outside scents John illustrated by talking about his Jamaican coffee: "The coffee is shaded by a pine forest. When you taste the coffee you can taste the pine."

John's trademark in the business is to find access to coffees that most other retailers don't find. His selection is limited, but of the highest possible quality, generally coming from small estates that produce a very limited amount of coffee. "There is magnificent coffee all over the world. Most of it goes to Japan and Europe, which means that the United States gets third pick." In his attempt to reeducate the American palate John hopes to turn this around, hoping that people will realize that "Coffee is like wine; there are so many good coffees in the world which we can't get, and we can't afford." It is the goal of J. Martinez & Co. to bring its customers a taste of these luxuries.

BOSTON STOKER
Bradford, Ohio

Sixteen years ago, Donald Dean owned a couple of cigar stores and kept a pot of high-quality coffee around for customers to enjoy. The coffee soon gained a popular following, and before long specialty coffee became part of the store's regular inventory. Ten years ago the coffee business became an even greater part of Boston Stoker's business, and Don began roasting his own beans and went wholesale with the results.

Today Boston Stoker has four locations throughout the Dayton, Ohio, suburbs, and although they still sell the finest cigars, specialty coffee has become such an integral part of the business that Don even dreams about coffee. Over the past sixteen years Don has seen tremendous changes in the market. "One of the greatest developments is decaf, and the decaf consumer is becoming increasingly more demanding. They want more selection, and the market seems to be responding because we are able to get a better selection ourselves." Don admits, however, that the decaf issue is very confusing. "Customers have a hard time trying to comprehend the actual processes. We sell both KVW and water process, but water process makes up 90 percent of our sales."

Another consumer trend he has noticed is the increasing sophistication of all clientele. "Customers in general are becoming more knowledgeable. They know what they're after. Although they are still price-conscious, it is our best products that are selling." This is evident even in the locations where there is largely a working class clientele. On week nights Don sees customers coming straight from the factory to walk out with $30 worth of coffee beans. "Although specialty coffee may have begun as an upscale product, every person has a product they love and are therefore willing to indulge extra money on. There may be more market resistance with specialty coffee because consumers are used to buying on price, but the working class is able to appreciate quality."

For himself, Don looks for coffees that display character, and he finds a lot of coffees to be exceptional. When pressed to name the coffee he would take with him to a deserted island, the choice as La Minita, a Costa Rican estate coffee. Kenyas and Javas received much praise also. He brews his favorite cup of coffee by dark-roasting La Minita and using a French-made Reneka espresso machine.

Roasting at Boston Stoker is generally darker than the area norms. A favorite blend is a combination of dark- and light-roast Java, and the best selling is a combination of three Central American coffees. The most important concept that Don Dean attempts to pass on to customers is that the quality of the bean going into the roaster, or into the blend, will determine the final product. He also feels that the greatest lack of consumer understanding is in this area. "Coffee is an agricultural product, and is therefore variable. The difficulty is in getting this across to someone who buys a specific coffee once, and then expects it to be the same every time."

Don Dean's love of the business stems from his original relationship with specialty coffee. "There is a mystique, a romance about coffee. When you have a cup of coffee with someone it reduces your apprehension. It makes you feel better about doing business with that person." He also states that he doesn't mind having "backed into" a business that seems to be continually expanding.

Dunn Bros. Coffee
St. Paul, Minnesota

Since the age of sixteen, Ed Dunn has been drinking coffee, but it was during a college stint as an "espresso jerk" that his interest with specialty coffee began. Ed started his coffee career in retail and moved through all the steps from roaster to green-bean buyer before opening Dunn Brothers Coffee in 1987. Although today he rarely gets to finish a cup, coffee is such an integral part of his everyday existence that he finds himself emptying green beans out of his socks before he goes to bed.

The specialty-coffee trade is still in its infancy in the St. Paul area, but Ed Dunn is out spreading the gospel of good coffee. The emphasis at Dunn Bros. is not only on quality coffee, but on information. Ed's awning above the door to his store sports the phrase, "Great java, no jive." What distinguishes his operation from others is that coffee is roasted every day in limited quantities. "While I may run out of some coffees and disappoint a few customers, I feel that running this risk is better than keeping thirty different kinds of roasted beans on the counter to go rancid. An added benefit is that the beans are still de-gassing when somebody takes them home. The resulting aroma lingers in the memory, as well as in the car, and may account for a noticeable percentage of repeat sales."

Ed does not have a general roasting philosophy. "Roasting depends entirely upon the individual coffee. A good example of this was a sundried Java which, after several experimental roasts, if it was roasted lighter than usual, turned out to have a wonderfully sweet flavor without being heavy-bodied. The one thing I do aim for is to take the beans through the roasting process slowly, particularly on dark roasts. These I finish without heat. It's a real challenge to push a dark roast without getting it too hot." Having experienced what he considers the definitive cup of coffee, a Jamaican Blue Mountain, Ed's favorite brew today is a dry-processed Ethiopian. "I like the gamey flavor of this coffee." Also on the top of his list is the San Sebastian Estate coffee from Guatemala.

"For people in this business the interest goes beyond profit. Like others, I am fighting all of the misinformation that exists. I don't sell water-processed decaffeinated coffees; instead I explain the KVW process to customers. When people listen they walk away feeling enlightened, and chances are they'll also walk away with the best-tasting decaf they've ever had. There is a tremendous potential for good decaf if the proper information is given." The impact of Ed's educational push has been pretty immediate. "Decaf coffee by Dunn Bros. has begun appearing on the menus of many of our restaurant accounts, which proves that people are interested in where the product comes from."

Another trend that Ed sees emerging is a movement away from alcohol. "Minneapolis is the treatment center of the United States. There are a lot of people who will drop by on their way to AA meetings. Young people are also making this move towards specialty coffee." Ed has noticed that there is a fondness for the unusual and ethnic. Considering the variety of origin and flavor that specialty coffee represents, it's no surprise that business is great for Dunn Bros.

McGARVEY COFFEE CO.
Minneapolis, Minnesota

Twenty years ago Douglas Carpenter was working for a commodities firm and searching for a job in a warm climate. During this job search he took time out to vacation in Minnesota and discovered Minneapolis's McGarvey Coffee. The quest for warm weather was quickly forgotten. "It was the vacation that turned into a vocation," Doug jokes. Today, he manages to combine his love of warm weather with visits to coffee-producing countries.

Doug immersed himself in the business. "When I first started working with McGarvey I used to ride the bus to work. Everyone on the bus used to look around to figure out who was drinking a cup of coffee. I was so saturated with coffee smoke and aroma that basically I had become a 170-pound coffee bean." In learning to view coffee as beverage rather than commodity, one of the most challenging things for Doug was to distinguish the nuances of taste in different coffees. He still spends a lot of time fine-tuning his palate. "Tasting is an ongoing process; I taste coffee every day from all over the world and I am constantly learning."

In the twenty years that Doug has been in the business, he has watched the trends in specialty coffee emerge. Several things stand out in his mind as important, and mostly positive, changes in the market. The only one that isn't an improvement is the demise of aged coffees. According to Doug, the trade doesn't carry aged coffees anymore because nobody can afford to keep them. Otherwise, the market has been full of improvements. "Twenty years ago there was no price fluctuation in the market. Exporters, importers, and roasters had to fight for every eighth of a cent. Today the situation is the opposite. Not only do you have to understand the product, but you have to be savvy in the marketplace. Fresh-roast decaf was also an unknown entity before 1980, and now it constitutes as much as 18 percent of our business."

But the most important change in the specialty-coffee market is that people are more aware of the product and are buying better coffee. "People's habits have changed, and their consumption has changed, but this has not always gone hand in hand with their awareness of what makes better coffee. Education has had to catch up with the public's changing tastes."

One of the most appreciated improvements at McGarvey Coffee was the arrival of valve packs, which allow gas to escape from packaged coffee beans without letting oxygen in. "Many people don't appreciate that they're dealing with a perishable product. Valve packaging allows us to pack coffee so that it has a shelf life."

Many of the questions that Doug's customers are asking today are directed at issues such as decaffeination. Doug deals with decaf carefully. "I look at decaf in terms of what tastes the best, and chemically decaffeinated has been best tasting." McGarvey offers both chemical and nonchemical products, because some customers don't want to deal with the subject of chemicals. "And after all," says Doug, "We're not chemists." While selling both chemical and natural decaf in the wholesale market, in the retail end of business McGarvey only offers naturally decaffeinated. "It is my hope to see the demise of chemically decaffeinated coffee. I always move towards the new technology, and wait for them to perfect it. Long term, you will wind up with a better product."

Concerning the other controversial trend in the industry, flavored coffee, Doug admits that some of his peer group doesn't love him. The view that Doug has taken is based on what he calls "absolute rational reason." He compares the flavored-coffee market to the wine industry. "People drank Kool-Aid with a kick ten years ago. Today, look at the growth in Cabernet and Chardonnay sales." Gourmet coffee is a taste, according to Doug, that the young consumer, especially, hasn't acquired. Flavored coffees provide an introduction into the market. "Our flavors are very good, because they're subtle. We scoured Europe before we decided what we wanted to buy." The result is five or six standard flavors that come from about six different flavor houses.

When tasting coffee, Doug takes into account body, flavor, and aroma. His favorite is Kenya AA. "I love the aromatic nature of this coffee. You can roast it dark and it will maintain its winey substance." He also loves to brew his "perfect cup" using the plunger method, because it produces the closest liqueur to cupping. But Doug admits that it's a lot more mess and fuss than most people are willing to deal with.

With roasting and blending, the key to success is unlocking flavor potential. This requires cupper evaluation. "You make the determination on how to roast the coffee by tasting it at a variety of roast shades." Doug points to a tendency of some retailers to roast too dark. "I think that this is for eye appeal." Blending for Doug is a marriage of flavors in which opposites like winey and mellow often attract. The trick to good blending then is in understanding how coffees balance one another.

A few final words on the subject from Doug include the recognition that everyone in the specialty-industry feels he or she has the best coffee. "Ultimately the beauty of coffee is in the eye of the beholder. People can always discover new and interesting coffees." What makes Doug qualify as an expert is experience. "It takes time to earn the 'silver spoon.'" Time needed to discover the nuances and subtleties that specialty coffee offers.

WILLOUGHBY'S COFFEE & TEA
New Haven, Connecticut

Barry Levine and Bob Williams opened their specialty-coffee store five years ago. Both of them had always bought specialty coffee, and were already in love with the end product. Earlier they were in a wholesale bakery business, so coffee drinking was a natural accompaniment. The switch into roasting and retailing specialty coffee gave them a chance to do what they liked best, manufacturing a product. They have since sold their other business and currently have one very busy store, with plans to expand, and an active mail-order business that allows customers to place orders via telephone, mail, or fax.

Their selection of roasts is based on three levels of darkness: full city, French, and Italian. Aware of the differences in vocabulary between the East and West coasts, Bob explains their roasts: "East Coast French roast is where oils come to the surface; it results in a bittersweet caramelized taste. Italian is black and oily. We currently offer six different French roasts, and our house blend is French roast." Their biggest seller is their house blend in full-city roast. Colombian and Guatemalan follow closely as favorites of the clientele.

Bob's personal favorites are Costa Rican and Kona. "The Kona peaberry is one of my all-time favorites. It roasts beautifully, looks gorgeous, and consistently tastes excellent." When brewing the perfect cup at home Bob uses a French plunger pot. "With the plunger pot you get fuller extraction. And I like a little sediment in my coffee as well as the coffee's oils." Barry agrees with the method. "I'm a plunger fan myself. I like the fact that nothing comes in contact with the coffee except water." But his favorite coffees are Kenya and true Yemen Mochas rather than Kona. Tips from Willoughby's on making the perfect brew at home include the following: "Use very fresh tap or bottled water. Grind beans directly before brewing. This is the single most important thing the coffee brewer at home can do."

The clientele demographics at Willoughby's has not changed much over the past five years, although Bob notes, "There are more grad students and faculty from Yale." He feels that part of the increase in academic consumers is due to Willoughby's dedication to education. "We publish a number of informational brochures. One on roasting variations, freshness of coffee, etc. even though a good percentage of consumers are already informed. A big part of the business is consumer awareness. Great coffee is an educational process. Anybody with any kind of sophisticated palate can't go back to canned coffee." Barry agrees with the importance of informing customers, and finds that at times it's a matter of "un-educating" them. "We are always trying to correct misinformation, teaching customers to unlearn ideas they've picked up form the mass marketing of commercial coffees."

Willoughby's offers three flavored coffees: hazelnut-vanilla, chocolate, and cinnamon. The flavors are also in decaf. "We flavor it all here. A grinder is dedicated solely to flavored coffees, and each flavor is scooped with its own scoop to avoid contaminating any of the other beans." Bob was quick to say, however, that they offer flavors "somewhat regrettably."

Willoughby's is committed to upgrading their decaf. "We used to offer Colombian in water- and chemical-decaf processes. Occasionally we'd have Sumatra. Now we have Ethiopian, Guatemalan Antigua, and Mocha-Java." Decaf accounts for about 18 percent of sales, and stays fairly steady. They still offer both kinds of decaf processes, and while customers occasionally have concern about methylene chloride, Willoughby's doesn't take a health stand, although, Bob says, "We will take a stand on taste differences of the two processes." Like many people in the business, Bob feels that water-processed decaf lacks full flavor.

Business is business; it concerns making a profit. But at Willoughby's it's also a labor of love. "We stand on freshness and quality. We turn over a lot of coffee; it comes out of the roaster and 99 percent of it is sold in a day or two." Their favorite part of the business is taking a project from conception, developing it, and nurturing it to finish. Roasting is the central part of this process. "Roasting, you become an extension of the roaster. You're an integral part of what's going on. All of the senses are involved in watching the beans expand and develop. It's a lot of fun." In Bob's opinion, "Great coffee involves the human eye." There is tremendous pride in the fact that Willoughby's is a state-of-the-art operation. "What we do can't be done any better. Duplicated, yes, but not improved upon. By and large," he explains, "we're lacking corporate mentality." But judging by their popularity, their customers don't miss it.

ALLEGRO COFFEE COMPANY
Boulder, Colorado

"You've got to pay your dues," say Jeff and Roger Cohn, brothers and coowner-operators of Allegro Coffee Company. "Over the years we've had dozens and dozens of people call us, some directly from producing countries and some claiming to have amazing connections or yet-untapped supplies for us to sample. But to date none of these solicitations have proven worthwhile. They've never turned out to be a reliable source of great coffee, no matter how much they've promised or how exotic their apparent find." The moral of the story? "We deal with established sources and suppliers we've come to trust over the years. These people have earned their reputations. And there just aren't any shortcuts—you've got to invest the time to know your coffee. There's no substitute for experience."

Experience has put the Boulder-based Allegro Coffee Company at the peak of the specialty-coffee trade throughout the Rocky Mountain region, an area stretching from the northern part of Colorado and following the Rio Grande past Santa Fe deep into the heart of New Mexico. The two brothers have also tested the waters in other regions and are now kept busy supplying their coffees to restaurateurs and retailers across the country.

Jeff and Roger Cohn started in the coffee business at tender ages, working summers at Superior Coffee, run by their father and uncle back in Chicago. Both have felt at home in the trade ever since.

In 1977, after several years of marketing specialty coffees for Superior, Jeff was the first to strike out on his own, opening two successful specialty retail shops in Boulder. Jeff explains: "I felt I could do more with a company whose raison d'être was based on the specialty-coffee product and its market, rather than working in a specialty department that was part of a large company with a broader focus. For me, the creation of Allegro Coffees represented that greater degree of specialization, that sharper focus on the highest-quality coffees."

Roger Cohn came on board with Allegro in 1982, where he has put his years of experience in coffee evaluation to their fullest use. As the resident coffee-tasting guru, Roger is also the one who travels to various producing countries such as Guatemala to inspect the coffee plantations themselves. That's where the emphasis on quality must begin.

The year Roger joined his brother in the Colorado company, Allegro began roasting its own gourmet coffees, and by 1985 it had established a considerable wholesale base—so much so that they sold the retail businesses and gave over all their energies to the rapidly expanding wholesale enterprise. This has taken them into supermarkets and independent groceries under a second brand name, Signature Coffee, in addition to the Allegro coffees sold to specialty retail stores, restaurants, and cafes.

Five years ago, Jeff and Roger also moved into the equipment end of business by importing espresso machines direct from Italy—a wise move since the current demand for these machines is outstripping supplies.

Do they have a favorite coffee at Allegro? Vail Blend, confessed Jeff, one of the Allegro Coffee blends specifically developed, with the help of the chef in residence, for a lodge in the ski resort that gives it its name.

LA CRÈME COFFEE & TEA
Dallas, Texas

Jerry and Bonnie Itzig began their venture in the specialty-coffee business six years ago by doing one thing: making espresso. "We put a roaster in the artist's district in town where there was no retail traffic, just a few offbeat art studios, and we roasted espresso." Jerry did all the roasting, and Bonnie did sales in the evening, going around to restaurants and asking people to compare the product with theirs. With the arrival of Southwestern cuisine people began to want the freshest-possible products. Consequently, clients began to ask the Itzigs to expand their lines of coffees. Both decided to take up the challenge. Bonnie says, "I tasted everything I could find, talked to everyone, and kept practicing." Jerry trained with various people, learning how to roast. Within three years La Crème tripled in size and had to move. Today they have not only a busy retail shop, but La Crème 1683, a European-style coffeehouse. Although both venues have been successful, the wholesale end is still vital to their success. Bonnie's heart is in the restaurants and hotels because they are the most challenging. She says, "People notice coffees when they go out, and that helps build business. Our retail and wholesale play off each other."

When Jerry and Bonnie began their business they found that people were not used to the more intense flavor of their product, even though, "our espresso was, and still is, a continental roast, not the dark Italian roast you find on the West Coast." Today, the market has become broader in its tastes and dark roast has become the standard. Their current biggest seller is, in fact, French roast. The other specialty at La Crème is the selection of flavored coffees. The response to these coffees has been amazing. Each restaurant account at La Crème has its own personal blend, and Bonnie spends hours mixing and remixing to get just the right combination. "I try to do more than just a coffee for my customers. I try to make it a recognizable part of their business, and something I am proud of, something that's uniquely theirs."

At home, Bonnie is still attached to their first love: she drinks only espresso at home. But as she explains, "Not just any espresso will do; it has to be good, good, quality beans. If it's simply a charred roast and not a good bean then the coffee's no good." (A note to tea-lovers: Jerry's drink is Yin Hao jasmine tea or ginger tea.)

The customer is important to the Itzigs, but they have found that not everyone wants to be educated. "You can tell a difference between a customer who wants to know, and who cares, from one who doesn't. There are some customers who will take their coffee home and blend it with Folger's," observes Bonnie. But she doesn't let this disturb her. They are optimistic that the quality of the product will eventually win out. But for wholesale accounts Bonnie has a very different philosophy. She has dropped restaurant accounts after finding out they were mixing La Crème coffee with a commercial brand. "I don't want people to associate La Crème with anything less than the best quality."

The Itzigs' philosophy embodies the community spirit that exists among people in the specialty-coffee business. Bonnie says, "I don't know that we're different from the competition. Everybody tries to roast as well as they can. I feel like everybody who's small is trying to do the same thing. We just try to be as honest as possible." What does set La Crème apart is their dedication to exploring new ideas. They're not just trying to build a market, they're trying to do different things. Innovation is the trademark of La Crème.

CAFFÉ LATTE
Los Angeles, California

Tom Kaplan was used to the good things in life, at least as far as food was concerned. His dad owns Hugo's, the first gourmet food establishment in the Los Angeles area. When Hugo's decided to make coffee, they wanted to make it the right way. Tom, who was in charge of selling all the exotic wares, went into research mode. In the process of finding better and better coffee, he ended up in San Francisco, where he found people roasting their own. This added a whole new dimension to the idea of fresh coffee, and Tom was soon roasting his own. In 1988 he opened Caffé Latte, a restaurant that revolves around a coffee roaster (see his recipe on page 204).

"Having the restaurant gives me the luxury of standing by my principles." These principles include not selling flavored coffee or Swiss water decaf. "Flavored coffee is either for stores who sell old coffee, or for stores that sell only tea and coffee and need to carry flavored in order to supplement their income." Swiss water lacks the flavor that Tom demands from his coffees. In decaffeinated coffee Tom hasn't seen much appreciable growth. "I personally don't care for it, but if I drank it I would drink the decaf Sumatra. Because Sumatra has a lot of body and oil to begin with, it tends to maintain flavor better." The restaurant is also a great vehicle for selling coffee. "People will have a great cup of coffee and want to take the beans home."

Roasting is an art form to Tom. "There is something really special about the perfect roast. I start every coffee differently. The way you start the coffee is the most important thing." All of his coffees are decidedly lighter than the average West Coast roast. One of Tom's secret agendas in the business is to wean people from their dark-roast coffees. "We don't carry a dark roast. Our French roast is lighter than probably anybody else's." He accomplishes the switching process with a 75 to 80 percent success rate. "I have people buy a blend of French roast and Sumatra, and then gradually increase the amount of the Sumatran."

"The growth of specialty coffee in this area is slow compared to other states because we have a lot of stores selling four-month-old coffee." Seeing more roasters in the city doesn't worry Tom; it makes him happy. "It's good for business. At this point there isn't any competition; it's just pioneers helping each other," he explains.

F. Gaviña & Sons
Vernon, California

Coffee has been part and parcel of the Gaviña family since 1870, when Pedro's grandfather farmed his own coffee plantation in Cuba. In the early 1960s, after the family moved to the United States, they took a short break from coffee, and in 1967 began Gaviña Coffee. Today, the company has expanded into all aspects of the coffee market. Their retail line, Don Francisco, can be seen in many major grocery chains, and they also supply to large wholesale accounts. The company is family owned and operated. Pedro's father, Francisco, although retired, still spends nearly every day at the company, keeping an eye on operations and offering advice.

Pedro's favorite coffee is Kenyan, and to make the perfect cup he uses the drip method, without any paper filter. "Paper does not allow coffee to extract properly, and other methods use too fine a grind. The fineness of the grind allows flavors you don't particularly want to be extracted. It also give the illusion of a stronger cup of coffee because of the bitterness. The best way to make a cup of coffee is not to skimp on the amount of coffee you use." Without question, however, the beverage of choice at Gaviña is espresso. "If there is good espresso around, I will always drink it rather than regular. In Cuba this is coffee to us; there is no other way of making coffee." For espresso, Pedro's favorite are the Central Americans. "Coffees such as Salvadors, Mexicans, and Brazils have less acidity. Espresso already brings out the acidity in coffees, and so these coffees better lend themselves to good espresso."

Over the more than twenty years that Pedro Gaviña has been in the coffee business, he has seen a lot of changes. "Coffee consumption in general has been on the decline since we've been in business. A lot of the blame for this lies with the commercial coffee industry, who in an effort to seem more cost-effective has come out with the idea of high-yield coffee. In the sixties people were urged to use close to a full ounce of coffee per cup. Today, with these 'high-yield' coffees, they don't use even half that. The consumer has lost the taste for coffee. It has become simply another beverage, which many people consume out of habit, rather than out of a desire for the taste."

Bringing specialty coffee to a larger market and educating people about what makes great coffee is the goal of Gaviña. To this end they have remained open to every new development in the business. Their operation is a marvel of new technology. Pedro was especially enthusiastic about valve packaging, which allows more people to get the taste of fresh coffee.

In their desire to offer their customers more choice, Gaviña sells three types of decaffeinated coffee—Swiss water process, direct process, and a new method that utilizes ethyl acetate—although, he observes, "There is not much of a concern regarding decaffeinated coffee which uses chemicals. In sales, we still do much more of our business in direct process." It is in the flavored coffees that Pedro has noticed a significant interest among consumers. "At least 5 percent of our total coffee sales are in flavored. In our retail sales that figure jumps to 20 percent. I personally do not drink flavored coffee, but I think that it is a terrific boost to the industry. Flavored coffees bring new people, especially the younger consumer, into the industry." What is important to the Gaviña family is what helps a customer develop a taste for specialty coffee, which they otherwise might never explore.

COFFEE EMPORIUM
Marina Del Rey, California

When asked what his relationship to specialty coffee was, Alan Chemtob replied, "Coffee is my life." His retail establishment in Marina del Rey grew out of a personal love of coffee. His grandfather was an importer who; among other things, brought in coffees from Colombia and Brazil. His own background was in the restaurant business. Alan began with a small coffee section in his cafe, but found that it was the retail part that drew customers in. Coffee became the center of the business and soon Alan was able to dedicate himself wholly to it. "I educated myself, bought a roaster, and taught myself to roast." The first attempts were not always successful, and, Alan admits, it was sometimes a hit and miss roasting process.

His roasting style developed from styles and philosophies he had read about. Today that style can be summed up as a process that develops a particular taste from the beans: what Alan refers to as a full roast, when oil is just beginning to appear, but before the point of carbonization.

The beans are a color between milk chocolate and semi-sweet. Of darker roasts Alan says, "You lose essences in dark roasting and over-roasting coffees. Roasting to a maximum, varietal flavor is lost because you've basically carbonized the sugars." So, at Coffee Emporium, each type of bean is roasted separately, and each varietal has a specific style. You won't find a Kenya dark roast and a Kenya light roast. You'll get Kenya at the optimum roast for its flavor characteristics.

With twelve years in the business, Alan has the distinction of being the first roaster-retailer in the L.A. area. He is also distinguished by having had the same roaster, Ricardo Sanchez, for eleven of those twelve years. Having the same person doing the roasting has helped to maintain a consistent style. There have been many changes in the industry during the time that Alan has been involved in it. Customers have changed, there are new competitors, and business has flourished. A significant part of the change is that people have become more educated. This is the result of a general rise in quality consciousness. "Orchestration of fine wines, cheeses, breads, growth in the fine-dining industry, celebrity chefs, you name it," Alan declares, "they have all helped sell specialty coffee."

Coffee Emporium also carries flavored coffees. They had no choice: flavored represents in the neighborhood of 20 to 25 percent of their business. Their decafs amount to as much as 25 to 30 percent of their business. They carry varietal decafs treated by KVW, the indirect water process. His clientele is concerned about chemicals, but, Alan says, "After a good explanation, customers don't worry."

When asked how he would choose a retailer, Alan's method was to separate those people who are in the coffee industry because they have passion for it from those who see it as a growth vehicle—franchisers, franchisees, etc.—who don't know much about the product. Why this important distinction? "If you have a passion for it, if you love not only the history but the growing, and flavor, the craft of coffee, then there is something that comes out of that which is a quality product; it has a style, a texture to it that makes it stand out," says Alan. Of course, Coffee Emporium is focused on that goal. "We like to differentiate our coffees, we don't mind experimenting, and we are flexible when it comes to people's tastes. We stand behind our product 110 percent."

Alan's personal preferences are good hearty coffees such as Kenya or blends. And he likes complexities. His brewing methods include Melior, and Toshiba drip for convenience. But his perfect cup requires more than adding the right amount of coffee to clean water. It must occur in the right environment. For Alan the right environment for a perfect cup of coffee is a nice little outdoor cafe in the south of France, in the company of a beautiful woman. But, as they say at Coffee Emporium, "The best coffee is the coffee you like best."

ALTA COFFEE
Newport Beach, California

If you don't know where Alta is, you could very well miss it. But chances are that if you stop and ask one of the locals, they'll be able to tell you exactly where to find it. From the outside the space they occupy resembles a warehouse, but it used to be a bookstore. (Visitors walk on a floor made of the former bookshelves.) Located on a little street in the beach community of Newport, Alta is a neighborhood institution. When you meet owners Patty Spooner and Tony Wilson, you soon realize why. Patty and Tony originally worked together at a mast-building company in Marina del Rey. On break, they would head over to the Coffee Emporium (see above) for a cup of their favorite brew. These coffee breaks inspired them with the idea for a new career after Patty and Tony were laid off. Five years later, they have a thriving coffee store and cafe.

Business at Alta is a cooperative effort, not only between Patty and Tony, but between them and their customers. Their cappuccino machine was bought in exchange for coffee from one of their restaurant accounts. Efforts to be environmentally conscious have resulted in customers bringing in their own mugs, which line the wall behind the counter. Education is an important part of customer service for Alta, and recycling is one of their pet projects. They have introduced unbleached filters, have begun composting used grounds and kitchen waste, and have even begun encouraging customers to bring in their own recyclables.

Issues of quality and freshness are more central to Alta than variety. They carry only a small number of the highest-quality coffees they can find, which are roasted French and Vienna style using a Sivetz roaster. What makes them stand out is the environment they have created. Fifty percent of the clientele are regulars, who come in and sit at the bar to chat.

In their own cups, Patty prefers a Costa Rican or Kenyan for the crisp flavor. Tony agrees on Kenyan as a favorite, but believes that coffee can taste different on a daily basis. If you're drinking a cup at Alta, whatever it is is sure to taste great.

DIEDRICH COFFEE
Tustin, California

The Diedrich family has an extensive (and impressive) involvement in specialty coffee. From farming and importing, to roasting and retailing, and even to manufacturing roasters, the Diedrichs have had a hand in it all. If there is genetic programming for the love of specialty coffee, this family has it. Martin Diedrich, once a machete-wielding archeologist and anthropologist, decided to join his family's coffee business in 1982. After a year and a half in apprenticeship with his father, Carl, he took over the retail business completely. That business now includes two extremely busy retail coffee bars and a national mail order business.

One of the things Martin has attempted to do is to develop a more diverse client base. At Diedrich Coffee, you'll find construction workers standing in line next to business men. The way that Martin manages to attract such a variety of customers is by providing better value for the dollar. "If you compare prices, we offer extremely high quality at an average cost of $8 a pound." The ability to offer great coffees at this price is one of the benefits of the extensive connections that come with being a Diedrich. The family began their interest in specialty coffee when Martin's father was growing some of the best coffee around in Antigua, Guatemala. While the family no longer owns a plantation, they have many grower friends who continue to supply them with high-quality coffee.

The roasting philosophy at Diedrich is based on maintaining as much control as possible over the beans. Part of this control involves roasting only in small batches. "Although it is very labor intensive, every coffee is roasted in the store, everyday," with a Diedrich coffee roaster, of course. Their proprietary roaster (see page 50) works on the principle of indirect heat and fast air cooling, and they sell it around the world. Get Martin to talking about the roaster, and you should plan on drinking more than a couple of cups of coffee.

The feeling you get at Diedrich's coffee is of being transported to another place, perhaps one near the coffee plantation where Martin grew up. "I had this idea to create an environment similar to Latin America. My store developed from my heart." Indeed, it reflects age-old traditions:

Spanish colonial architecture, a bright tile mosaic, and as in the houses of Guatemala, a feeling that every object in the room comes from the earth.

Because Martin's name is so well known and his stores are so successful, there is a constant flow of would-be coffee retailers through the stores.

When it comes to specialty coffee Martin feels that the roasters and retailers in America are setting the trends. "We're the role models, not the Europeans," he states.

Martin's own preferences in coffee change frequently, although he never drinks espresso or French roast. "I don't like espresso because it's over too quickly." Martin likes the fine subtleties of coffee, and spends time making his customers aware that different methods extract different flavors from it. For his own coffee drinking, however, he most frequently uses the drip method. A great coffee to Martin embodies the ambiance of its country. "Coffee is a living, organic thing. It should be full of life."

KELLY'S COFFEE FACTORY
Long Beach, California

Six years ago, Terry Kelly had a successful candy company that was enticing people into the store with its delicious fudge—made the old-fashioned way on a thick marble slab and cooked in a spun-copper kettle—along with its fresh-baked cinnamon rolls. To help capture the morning market, Kelly's started serving coffee, but they wanted to do it right.

Doing it right meant learning about beans from the time they were green to the time they were ground. They put their first roaster into their Long Beach store and began roasting their own beans. Their roasting style envelops a gamut of roasts. Terry maintains that each roast should cater to the individual coffee, but there is a need to generalize. Zimbabwe's, for example, will always roast a little longer. Roasts are done in small batches, five to ten pounds, which Terry says is a difficult practice for a business to maintain. The goal at Kelly's is to maintain good body and balance.

Kelly's currently has thirteen locations, from Missouri to California, and plans another seven by year's end. Most are located in regional shopping and theme centers, and all offer Kelly's famous original fudge. "Specialty coffee is tied in with all of our products," explains Terry. "So much, in fact, that Kelly's is now the largest coffee roaster in Orange County." The goal at Kelly's is, as Terry says, "to cater towards the gourmet, not just serve a cup of coffee." Attaining this goal comes through promotions such as offering gourmet cups of the day in some of their locations. "You can get a cup of Jamaica Blue Mountain, Kona, or La Minita at many of our stores." Their St. Louis stores were the first to introduce cappuccino to the area.

Decaffeinated is kept to a minimum at Kelly's. "To make sure decaf is fresh, we have the stores only order four to five bags at a time, and have them keep the inventory as low as possible." The reason for such cautious supply is that they've found customers are concerned about process, and therefore sales are slow. "People need to be educated," explained Terry. Kelly's doesn't carry Swiss-water-process decaf because they've found that its taste doesn't measure up to its price.

The perfect cup of coffee for Kelly's is something exotic; Tanzanian or Zimbabwe. The recommended brewing method is one that saturates the grounds thoroughly. For this reason they like the French press, although they realize that this is a messy process and takes some getting used to.

The quality of the green beans is the most important thing to Kelly's. And maintaining that quality all the way through to the final cup means taking such extra precautions as a water filter system at each store. Kelly's is a place with no secrets. The coffee, like the candy, is made right out front. And many of the customers find that one of the more enjoyable pastimes is to sip their Jamaican Blue and watch caramel apples being dipped, or to smell hot cinnamon rolls as they're pulled from the oven.

SEE'S COFFEE
Riverside, California

Lydia See was working in the Napa Valley, and had been actively involved in restaurant management for a number of years, when she was asked to serve as a consultant in the planning of a new coffee store. She soon realized that the coffeehouse experience incorporated the best of what she had liked about the restaurant business, but was a lot simpler. The idea for See's Coffee had been planted, and in 1987 Lydia began the process that would make it a reality. See's Coffee opened its doors in 1988 in Riverside. Today a second store is under construction in Santa Barbara, and plans for a third are developing quickly.

Lydia's original enthusiasm for the coffee business is still present in her store today. "I've found the coffee scene to be something that lifts people, and so my customers are pleasant. They have a different attitude when they walk into the store because they are treating themselves to something special." She expects this enthusiasm to be reciprocated on the other side of the counter, "All of my employees love coffee and everything that the cafe involves. If they don't, they don't work here."

Roasting is done on the premises almost every day and the batches are kept small. Lydia's involvement with the process of roasting is complete, and she'll get right on top of the roaster in order not to miss a thing. "I am into the feel, the sight, the sound, and the aroma that roasting involves. I think there is a beauty to the roast as it goes through different stages and colors." Getting the perfect roast at See's involves every one of the senses. "After hearing the first crack I judge the roast by its color. Most importantly, I know my beans and their moisture content. I know just before they're going to crack." This noise, which to the outsider sounds something like popcorn crackling, sends Lydia some important information. "The prettier the crack, the better the taste, in my experience."

Because of her complete involvement in the roasting process, Lydia doesn't carry water-processed decaf. "I won't roast water process because you don't get that pretty color or crack ever. I believe that the oils are washed out of the beans in this process, and much of the flavor along with them." For Lydia, this means that in the cup the taste doesn't measure up and the aroma is too weak. If queried by customers about health factors, Lydia is firm. "I truly believe that there is no residue. All the chemicals are burnt out before the coffee is in the cup." So for now See's carries what Lydia considers the best-tasting decaf available, KVW, a direct-processed decaf. But she's excited about other options, such as CO_2.

Asked about flavored coffees, Lydia replies, "I had originally intended to carry only three flavors. Today I probably carry sixteen as a result of bringing in flavors customers requested." Because she doesn't drink the flavored coffees herself, she continues to rely on her customers' tastes in this area.

What does make it into Lydia's cup changes with time. "Currently, I love Indonesias, specifically the Javas. Though, the Guatemalas are real nice too." She brews her favorites "by the cup!" But on the occasions that call for making coffee by the pot she recommends brewing into a thermos that will keep the coffee hot without becoming stale. "We have a lot of lousy coffeemakers on the market, and they can make the best fresh specialty coffee taste bad." Her strongest recommendation for great coffee is "Don't let your coffee sit on a burner."

It's obvious that Lydia loves the end product, but what keeps her excited about the business is the social scene that revolves around her store. "I'm not just a roaster and a specialty-coffee dealer; we have music here five nights a week." By offering a lot of outdoor seating, See's Coffee caters to the diverse group of teachers, professionals, and students who gather there alone with a book or with a group of friends. "Many people tell me the store reminds them of Europe," says Lydia. To accompany its coffee, See's offers crisp biscotti and muffins.

Lydia sees her clientele becoming increasingly sophisticated and consisting more and more of younger coffee drinkers. This youthful trend means a growing popularity of nonalcoholic coffeehouses, and a booming business for See's. Between plans for the new stores, poetry readings, live music, and roasting every day, Lydia wants to begin a mail-order business. It seems as if she has ventured into almost every aspect of the coffeehouse scene, but she keeps things in perspective. "I feel pretty young in the business, and there's so many other things I'm finding out. I'm still in the process of learning."

THE COFFEE ROASTER
Sherman Oaks, California

In the late 1960s, Dick Healy was a long way from Sherman Oaks. Stationed in Central America as a naval advisor, he was enjoying the beautiful highlands of Guatemala and Costa Rica, and learning to love great coffee. When he returned to the United States he found a new career in banking, but couldn't find good coffee anywhere. "I was disappointed with the coffee that I got here. In fact, I found commercial coffee undrinkable." Unwilling to give up his beloved beverage, Dick roasted coffee at home for himself and friends. Three years ago, he decided to go public. "When I decided to get out of the banking world, it was a natural to move into the coffee-roasting business." Today, Dick's store in Sherman Oaks, the Coffee Roaster, is testimony to his longstanding love of the brew.

At the Coffee Roaster, the actual roaster seems a natural part of a place dedicated to great coffee and everything necessary to enjoy it. Refreshingly free of polished metal and extraneous glitz, everything about the Coffee Roaster speaks of comfort, including the freshly baked blueberry muffins. At 7 a.m., Dick is already well into his daily roasting chores. Roasting, as Dick describes it, is entirely subjective. "I try to roast each coffee to what I personally feel is its peak flavor. In this way it's very much an art." Dick doesn't believe in hurrying the roasting process, but avoids what he calls "baking the coffee." Instead, he nurtures the roast along, searching for the greatest depth and intensity of flavor. "The degree of roast will vary slightly depending on the coffee's origin or even the particular lot of green coffee," he explains.

Dick holds strong opinions about decaffeinated coffees. He currently only carries the direct-process method by KVW. "I've tried all the processes—Swiss water, CO_2—and they either aren't up to my standards, or else they don't provide the flavor of KVW."

As for all the fuss about flavored coffees, Dick remains neutral. Although he agrees that flavored coffees are a West Coast trend, he keeps in mind that they also have a history. While flavored coffee doesn't make its way into Dick's cup, it has made it onto the Coffee Roaster's shelves. Flavored coffee accounts for 10 percent of sales, but Dick remarks, "I sell more Italian roast than all of my flavors combined." One of the reasons that Dick sells more dark roast than flavors might be that his clientele has educated tastes. He has taken the time to know his neighborhood and his customers, and they make up what he considers the perfect specialty-coffee clientele. "My customers tend to be in a higher socio-economic group, and they're older, between thirty and fifty." For this reason, also, Dick rarely finds himself having to tell people how to brew their coffee, but gets to enjoy discussions on such subjects as Guatemala's current crop, and differences in regional coffees. He encourages his customers to experiment, and will gladly sit down and sample a variety of coffees with anyone who's interested.

For Dick Healy, going to work every day is like going to a party. "I'm around something which gives me immense pleasure." Although many of his business friends might have thought him crazy to go into a retail business, Dick feels he's gained immeasurably from it. "I've become even more optimistic about people since I opened. My customers are magnificent." But if you're looking for the Coffee Roaster Two to open in your neighborhood, you have a long wait. "I do a thriving mail-order business, but I'm not going to open more stores. There is plenty of room in the business for everyone."

MOUNTANOS BROS. COFFEE COMPANY
San Francisco, California

In the thirties a Greek immigrant by the name of Richard Mountanos sold roasted coffee and chestnuts from a don-key-drawn cart in Washington, D.C. There was concern among some of the politicians that this didn't suit the dignity of the Hill, and he was asked to move. At that point President Franklin D. Roosevelt stated, "As long as I'm in office, the Greek on the corner stays." It seems the president liked fresh-roasted coffee. It also seems that the Mountanoses liked roasting coffee, because they've become one of the most established names in the specialty-coffee business. Today, Mike Mountanos is carrying on the same traditions of consistent quality and innovation that made his family famous. His story begins in 1981, after the company his grandfather started had changed hands. There was no question but that Mike was going to remain in coffee. "I was born into coffee," he exclaims.

Mountanos Brothers is a wholesale coffee business that supplies fresh-roasted coffee to a number of retail coffee outlets, small and large. The emphasis at the company is on the roasting process, which Mike says depends on an intuitive sense of timing. This special feel for when a roast is at its peak comes from years of practice. The company uses a redesigned Jabez Burns roaster, which is an indirect-fired roaster. "The flame shoots into the middle of the drum, and there is a constant flow of air in the machine so that the coffee is never exposed to the recirculation of gases." This continual flow of air is a significant factor in the taste of Mountanos's coffee. "Our coffee is clean tasting, and sweeter," says Mike. Roasting is accomplished in the shortest period of time possible, which, Mike explains, allows the moisture in the coffee to be driven out, and the bean to develop color from the inside. When the bean reaches a dark brown color and oil begins to show on the surface, the roast master determines the critical moment to release the beans into the cooler in order to maintain consistency from batch to batch. This is an art that can only be passed on from generation to generation, from roaster to roaster, over many years. The coffees at Mountanos Brothers are often described as having a "cleaner" taste. Custom mechanical additions to the roasting machines are given credit for this, because they allow tighter control over when the roasting process stops.

Mike's favorite coffees when he's brewing up a cup are Sumatra and Colombian. "I love Colombian because it's so versatile, and lends itself to several ways of roasting."

One of the subjects sure to set Mike to grinding his teeth is the profusion of labels reading "gourmet coffee." "The term 'gourmet' is overused in the marketplace, and improperly used as well. Webster's defines *gourmet* as a person who enjoys fine things, not a thing that is special. Only 10 percent of the total market is real specialty coffee," Mike points out. "There's just not enough high-quality coffee in the world." To counter this kind of advertising, Mike spends hours in what I think of as his laboratory. Much like a scientist, Mike spends hours sample roasting and tasting different beans to try and find the right combination of highest-quality *arabica* coffees to enable him to merchandise canned ground specialty coffee.

Michael's goal is to get the public to realize that great coffee exists. If some consumers can't be weaned away from the convenience of cans, this may be the only way to get them to drink the real thing. If anyone is prepared to take on the challenges involved in such a concept, it's Mike, and he'll no doubt succeed.

As for decaffeinated coffee, Mike has noticed a tapering off in the consumption of the water-processed variety. He feels that this is due to a more educated consumer, whose interest is in taste. "My personal preference is the FDA-approved methylene chloride because it gives superior taste, but I see a portion of the market moving towards CO_2."

Mike has a variety of flavored coffees, all of them flavored at the plant. "We're very careful to keep the flavored coffees specially packaged and separated from our other coffees." As for the debate over offering flavored coffees, Mike feels that he's in business to give his customers the best of what they want. "If you really like a coffee, you should be allowed to enjoy it."

THE COFFEE CRITIC
San Mateo, California

Linda Nederman-Mountanos, owner of the Coffee Critic in San Mateo and Burlingame, was introduced to specialty coffee six years ago, after meeting Mark P. Mountanos, a fourth-generation coffee merchant (see above). On that first evening, she remembers drinking no less than eight cups of freshly roasted Celebes Kalossi. She was an instant convert, and today she is married to Mark and in the coffee business to bring others that same sensation she experienced years ago.

Her store is a testament to the fact that she loves what she does. Her walls are covered with charts and wall-sized murals depicting coffee history both factual and folkloric. Her shelves are lined with antique coffee containers, and there are usually stacks of informational pamphlets for customers to take home. In Linda's opinion, "Refining the public's knowledge is the first step to refining their taste buds." For Linda the reward comes when customers begin to realize that coffee, like fine wine, should be savored and enjoyed, not hastily consumed and forgotten about.

The offerings at the Coffee Critic are extensive. Linda and "the Coffee Critic crew" emphasize education and experimentation to the public. She says, "I have access to almost any type of coffee my customers want." Daily roasting is done in small batches to maintain quality and to ensure the freshness of her product. Linda's roaster sits in the front of her store, where she can be available to chat with customers in between roasts. It's this combination of craftsmanship and public contact that makes Linda love the business. It's more than just offering the freshest and highest-quality coffee: it is creating an atmosphere. "Consistency is one of the keys to success. People know they will always get the best cup of coffee available when they come here," she says, "but they also know they have a place where they can meet for a lively discussion."

PEET'S COFFEE & TEA
Emeryville, California

The "gourmet revolution" of the seventies and eighties, according to many who studied the trend, started with a small restaurant in Berkeley, California, called Chez Panisse, which opened its doors in 1971. But if the revolution truly did start in Berkeley, the first shot was fired five years earlier around the corner from the restaurant at Peet's Coffee & Tea.

Opened by Alfred Peet, a Dutchman with particular tastes and an unwavering sense of quality, Peet's Coffee & Tea has defined specialty coffee in the San Francisco Bay Area for three decades. (Alfred Peet has since retired and is a much-quoted coffee expert.) Competitors in the Bay Area to this day complain that if they don't roast in Peet's style (dark), most of their customers will not believe that the coffee even approaches top quality.

But roast style, while it may be the most obvious characteristic of Peet's coffees, is only part of the story. Peet's has always been committed to buying the best-quality coffees available and has often been the first to import many particular coffees that later became famous throughout the specialty trade.

The philosophy at Peet's is that coffee should be good but not expensive. Because of the high volume the stores have developed over the years, Peet's owners can afford to sell their coffee at relatively low prices and still use top-quality coffees.

This no-nonsense approach is consistent throughout the Peet's stores and in their products. Flavored coffees will never be sold at Peet's, and it is unlikely that customers will be able to purchase fancy coffees from particular estates—or at least they won't be told they're doing so. While Peet's often buys the fanciest coffees available from a given part of the world, they don't like to say which exact farm they come from. They feel that their ability to select and roast are more important factors than which coffee they are using. As a variable agricultural product, no one coffee is ever the best, and by not identifying which coffees they're using, the people at Peet's feel they have more latitude to select the best they can for their customers.

One of the people responsible for quality control at Peet's is Jim Reynolds, the green-coffee buyer. According to Jim the acidity of a given coffee is of the utmost importance to him. The dark roast takes away a lot of the acidity and the more floral aspects it may have, and only a high-grown, well-prepared coffee can withstand the rigors of a dark roast and still retain its varietal character. While some coffee professionals might argue that a dark roast allows the roaster to use practically any coffee and still get the same flavor, the people at Peet's feel just the opposite is true.

Peet's, first founded in the heart of one of America's most rebellious communities of the sixties, set in motion its own revolution when it set about to redefine coffee to the American public. Today they are regarded in the trade as one of if not the first roasters of good coffee in the country—not the kind of coffee to be worshipped, like rare wine, but to be regularly appreciated, like a good friend.

LION COFFEE
Honolulu, Hawaii

Lion Coffee was originally formed in the 1860s in Toledo, Ohio. In its heyday it was the second-largest coffee roaster in the United States. After its demise, the company became well known in the antiques trade for the cards, dolls, sheet music, and other printed materials it had created as giveaways. For Jim Delano, Lion Coffee represented the perfect combination. With his background as an art student, Jim became fascinated with Lion Coffee's printed materials. As a lover of cafe culture, he also had a strong interest in the product. In 1979, Jim bought the remains of Lion Coffee, including its distinctive stern-faced trademark, and began Lion Coffee in Honolulu, complete with cards, paper clips, and other giveaways in the Lion tradition. "We have our own in-house art department which we affectionately call the Ministry of Fun. One of the things which distinguishes Lion Coffee is that we add that quotient of fun to every cup of coffee."

What began as three or four people behind the counter of a downtown coffeehouse has blossomed into a more-than-lucrative wholesale business. Lion coffee is distributed in most of the large supermarket chains and at many retail and military outlets. Their mail-order business is also expanding rapidly. Many of their mail-order clients are people who have visited Hawaii on vacation and have acquired a taste for the Lion. Jim attributes the popularity of the Lion's mail-order division to the fact that you can buy pineapples in Minneapolis, but you can't buy Lion Coffee.

Jim learned the artistic part of his business by majoring in art history, but the coffee part came differently. "I learned by visiting a lot of people in the business. I asked what they liked and what they felt was good. Then I spent a lot of time listening to customers." One of the important rules Jim learned is still followed today. "We don't categorize coffee into right and wrong. There isn't one perfect way to brew, or one perfect coffee."

For himself, Jim prefers variety. "I like to try all the different versions. I brew coffee in every possible way. Most of the time this means using a Melitta single-cup filter. Automatic drip rarely has as good a flavor. I also use the cold-water process, especially for iced coffee. And I like espresso, too." In his search for variety, Jim is always asking customers what they do at home. He's had some pretty surprising answers. "There was one customer who told me he blended instant coffee with his regular coffee." This was one taste variety that Jim didn't care to repeat at home. Other inspirations have come from the employment applications at Lion Coffee. One form question asks the applicant to relay his or her experiences with coffee. Stories have included coffeepots exploding, and attempts to use paper towels as filters. But a fellow applying for a job in the quality-control lab supplied Jim with one of his favorite stories. "He had invented an elaborate coffee-brewing process, using distilled water. It took him something like two hours to brew a pot of coffee." His experimentation and interest has provided Jim with the belief that the simplest methods work best. His advice on how to make the perfect cup is to look for high-quality beans. "For myself it's important that the coffee be really fresh." One thing Jim indulges himself in is brewing fresh coffee on airplanes. "I bring my own coffee and one-cup filter and ask the flight attendants to provide the hot water. I usually wind up making cups for them while I'm at it." As for the kinds of coffee he drinks: "I rarely drink the same coffee more than one day in a row. I probably drink ten coffees a week. Most of the time, however, I tend to prefer Kona, or Central American. But not roasted too dark. I like to taste the different acids and flavor components. And I brew it very strong."

All the decaffeinated coffee at Lion is processed by the KVW direct method using methylene chloride. "I've tried a lot of different kinds," explains Jim, and he has chosen the decaf with the best flavor.

Based on his clientele and their concerns, Jim believes that American food has changed tremendously over the last few years, and that people are much more discriminating. "We've spent a lot of time educating our customers. By doing this we hope we are helping customers determine what coffees fit their preference." High quality and the best possible taste are important to most consumers, and this is why the specialty-coffee industry has been so successful. Specialty coffee is one of the few markets in which a large number of small companies has been successful. Jim wants the market to stay this way. "I hope people don't buy into the advertising that the large companies can produce the same thing as someone who is overseeing the entire process. We communicate what our brand is by small things. We don't bludgeon people with advertising." Coffee to this king of the jungle is more than a cup of hot and black: it's a beverage with a rich history, its own culture, and an ability to give great pleasure to those who love it.

THE KOBOS COMPANY
Portland, Oregon

David Kobos and his wife were New York City teachers who loved good food. Teaching in the lower East Side allowed them to explore Chinese, Spanish, and Italian markets. Their appreciation of food extended to their morning cup. "We purchased coffees at Zabar's and Schapira Bros. and became coffee fanatics while we were cooking our way around the city," remembers David.

In 1972 the Kobos's moved to Portland in order to raise a family and start a specialty store of their own. In 1973 they turned their hobby into a business and opened a gourmet cookware and coffee store. "I bought a Probat twelve-kilo machine and started roasting right in the store." This practice continued for the first ten years, and made the Kobos Company a unique spot. Today things have changed a little. When they first opened they were the only coffee store within the Portland city limits; now there are about thirty, not counting grocery stores, and five of those do their own roasting.

So what sets Kobos apart? "We're unique in our mix. We have gourmet cookware and gadgets in half our stores. We do a very expensive job on coffee accessories. We carry all the espresso and drip machines. Many coffee places don't play this end of the retail game." The success they've enjoyed in retail has led Kobos to expand. Today he has six stores and a booming wholesale business. The restaurant accounts took off two years ago, and they have over sixty now. David credits the break in wholesale to consumers who are more quality-conscious. Restaurant customers have begun to demand a decent cup of coffee after dinner. Education and information about coffee has become important to the retailer who wants to be successful in today's market. As David remarked, "Consumers today are more and more sophisticated. In order for them to come to us, rather than the grocery store, we have to have better and better quality, and they have to be able to notice the difference."

Not only is his clientele more demanding, but over the years David has noticed that its range has grown wider, and that younger people now are drinking coffee. This is shown by the boom in espresso bars. Everybody, it seems, is drinking espresso drinks. The espresso trend is a welcome one to Kobos, who feels that one of the biggest problems of the coffee trade is that it has failed to draw younger drinkers. "We need to find ways to introduce younger people to the joy of the beverage. We can't expect them to go straight into espresso. They need to start with cream and sugar, or lattes." For the same reason, Kobos feels that finding the best possible decaffeinated and flavored coffees is important, although his entry into this segment of the market has been conservative. Kobos uses direct method solvent-processed decafs for the most part, although they do have a couple of Swiss-processed water decafs. Taste is the deciding factor for Kobos, "We only use KVW, because in the cup nothing else comes close; ethyl acetate and CO_2 just don't compare." In choosing flavors for coffees, he listens to his customers. "Generally we mix about five varieties, and we try to turn over every coffee within a week."

Kobos is a true connoisseur of freshness. At home he grows three acres of vegetables, and raises a selection of livestock. He drinks a variety of coffees, many of them estate coffees. "I love the estate Kenyas, and from Guatemala I love the San Sebastian. Arabian Mocha, Celebes, Sumatra Mandheling—it varies. I go in phases. Every once in a while I get a great Colombian that I really like, and every few years Kona is good. I had a Jamaican a few years ago which was every bit what it should be. Today, this is true of Yergachefs, the heavy, syrupy aged Mandhelings." As you can tell, David is enthusiastic about his products. He is also cautious of unnecessary tampering, and prefers to blend with great caution. "I've never been into creating a whole line of blends. We've done it for the restaurant trade because what works for a home machine doesn't always work for a restaurant."

When roasting these great coffees, David lets his palate be his guide. He works to avoid baking coffee and to maintain consistency. He cups all coffees and then tries to pick an optimum point of roasting for each one. And each coffee is indeed different: the Sumatran is given a Vienna roast, which develops the bean to a point where it is just beginning to oil up. The Celebes is roasted to a state between their regular (full-city) roast and a Vienna. And then Centrals are roasted right to the point of oiling.

After eighteen years in the business, David Kobos is still excited about coffee. "The most appealing thing about the business is the excitement of dealing with a commodity. Coffee is so full of romance, and there are so many stories behind each coffee."

CARAVALI COFFEES
Seattle, Washington

After graduating from college in 1979, Tim McCormack spent his time answering want ads in the Seattle newspapers. This occupation that eventually led him to Starbucks Coffee Company and a growing love of specialty coffee. Today he is the driving force behind Caravali Coffees. (Caravali was originally created in 1984 as the wholesale division of Starbucks Coffee, and in 1987 it became an independent company.)

Tim's success in the specialty-coffee business is tied in with his commitment to a roasting philosophy. At Caravali, coffees are roasted "full city," or to the point where the oil is just beginning to bead on the bean. As he explains, "There are attractive flavors on both sides of the roasting spectrum. Lighter roasting, however, can produce a heavy, sour, or coarse pungency associated with high acidity. Darker roasting will often result in a burnt, bitter, or acrid smoky flavor. Full city, when it's done properly, brings out in coffee the chocolate, cinnamon, and nutmeg flavor notes. It defines the 'sweet spot' in the middle.

"One of the things that I've found is that consumers confuse the issue of strength versus dark roast. They associate the burnt flavor of a French roast with 'strong' coffee." At Caravali coffee, when they roast French roast, it is allowed to coast to a finish. The burners are cut off as soon as the beans reach a full-city roast, and then thermal momentum finishes the roasting process, a method that keeps less-pleasant flavors to a minimum.

When asked about various coffees, among them the well-known Jamaica Blue Mountain and Kona, Tim replied that his own favorite coffee is Estate Java. "Jamaica Blue Mountain is nicely balanced, but for the most part over-rated. Kona, likewise, is more of a marketing phenomenon than a truly great coffee. While some of the estate coffee from Kona is worth taking note of, most of the time you don't know what you're getting. I think the best coffee produced in the western hemisphere is Finca San Sebastian from Guatemala's famed Antigua region."

Blending at Caravali takes place both before and after roasting, and is one of Tim's favorite occupations. "I get very excited about blending. There is so much subtlety to it, which comes out when you begin to cup and sample. Proportions are constantly changing in our blends, and we find ourselves adding smaller quantities of more coffees to achieve specific results."

When asked about the flavored coffees at Caravali, Tim referred to the historical perspective. "Coffees have been flavored with nuts, chocolate, and spices since the beverage first began to be enjoyed. I'm very proud of the flavored coffee we produce. We listen to our customers." And the clientele, in his opinion, is getting more savvy. "There is more demand for information. The consumer today is willing to pay for quality."

One of the most commonly asked questions regarding flavored coffees is whether artificial or natural flavoring is used, on which Tim comments: "There is as much confusion about flavorings as there is about decaffeination. The concern that makes people tend to prefer a product labeled 'natural' is similar to the one that directs people towards water-processed decafs. The issue is over solvent residues on the product, but in fact no one has ever found residual solvent in a cup of decaffeinated coffee. By the same token, not all natural flavorings are better for you than artificial ones, and in some cases they are absolutely identical. It is really a larger issue of the perception of risk. People are threatened by things which they can't see and therefore can't control." In order to better serve all their clients, Caravali carries both water-processed and solvent-processed decaf. Decafs make up a solid 20 percent of their business today.

For brewing purposes, Tim swears by the French-press method. "The plunger pot keeps the brew colloids intact. Besides, I don't care for the taste of paper filters." The ultimate coffee for Mr. McCormack? "Proper espresso is the ultimate coffee."

TORREFAZIONE ITALIA
Seattle, Washington

For almost fifty years the Bizzarri family has been involved with coffee. Originally from Perugia, Italy, the Bizzarris have reemerged in Seattle. I spoke with Emanuele Bizzarri, the third generation to work in the coffee business, about their two unique retail stores. "My father is the roast master of the business. He learned his trade from my grandfather, who roasted coffee in Italy prior to the advent of big business taking over the roasting industry." In the United States for four years now, the family still maintains their link to Italy. Everything in the store is Italian, including the roaster, a Vittoria from Bologna.

Besides this European flair, something else makes Torrefazione unique. Unlike most specialty-coffee retailers, they don't offer individual estate coffees; all the coffees they sell are blends. "We sell two light-, two medium-, and two dark-roasted coffees. All of them a different blend. Three years ago my father took samples from all different brokers, trying all different mixes and roasts. These blends are my father's creation." At Torrefazione straight is not the way; they feel that most things in the world need mixing. This doesn't apply, however, to flavored coffees. "We don't do flavors. Coffee should be drunk for itself, the way that it is."

Unlike Europe, Emanuele feels that there's a big market in the United States for decaffeinated coffee. Since much of the original flavor can be lost in the decaf process, Torrefazione roasts their decaf a bit darker to maintain the coffee's flavor.

Emanuele's advice concerning espresso is: "If you're going to buy an espresso machine, spend the money and get a good one." His own favorite is the commercial San Marco espresso machine. Espresso is his drink, and when asked what coffee he uses, his answer was "good coffee." But asked to name a favorite kind, he says he likes "Perugia," one of Torrefazione's special blends. As for his customers, he says, "I tell people try a little of everything." How does he make his coffee at home? "I am always at the shop so I don't drink coffee at home. While I'm here I drink probably twenty cups of espresso a day."

STARBUCKS COFFEE COMPANY
Seattle, Washington

Starbucks Coffee is one of the best examples of the growth of specialty coffee among today's quality-conscious consumers. At this writing there are sixty-three company-owned stores from Chicago to Portland, with more to come. The phenomenal growth of Starbucks presents a number of challenges, especially since their mottos are "Be exact in labeling and information," and "Be proud of every product that goes out the door."

Vice-President Dave Olsen grew up in Montana. While visiting San Francisco he was introduced to Peet's coffee by friends, and had a chance to visit the small cafes in North Beach. The combination of the two was enough to trigger a desire for great coffee on a regular basis, and in 1975 he opened Cafe Allegro near the University of Washington (which he still owns and operates) and became Starbucks's first important espresso account. Today, along with his assistant Kevin Knox, Dave buys all the coffee for the Starbucks operations. Cupping is done on a regular basis, not only by Dave, Kevin, and the roasters in the corporate offices, but as part of the employee training throughout the company. Customers are kept aware of new blends, crops, and harvests by flags on boards on the wall above the counter, which list available coffees. The company's awareness of the seasonality of this product is so keen that a wake was held when the last of the Yemen Mochas made their way out of the corporate offices last year.

The people at Starbucks hold strong opinions on the issues of decaf and flavored coffees. None of the stores carries flavored coffee. "Flavored coffee is an undergraduate education for the specialty-coffee consumer, and that education can be had elsewhere," says Olsen. While stores carry both chemically and water-processed decaf coffees, only the chemical-process coffees are brewed in the store. "Safety and cup quality are our main concerns when it comes to decaf. We feel that chemically decaffeinated coffee offers the best of both worlds, but we offer Swiss water process as a service to our customers who feel differently," Dave explains. Accepting that customer opinion may differ from corporate opinion is central to Dave's idea of what makes a successful specialty-coffee business: "We must make coffee more accommodating. We can't take a product-centered notion. We have to be more user friendly, dropping negatives about dictating what people want."

When asked about roasting and blending, both Dave and Kevin come alive, pulling out charts and describing the different blends. "Ultimately what we're after is immediate, unquestioning enjoyment. We use a full-city roast, which is a shade darker than most roasters, but which we feel attenuates acidity slightly. In lighter roasts the acidity becomes the only dimension of the coffee you experience. Of course, the balance you strive to achieve is specific to each particular coffee or blend." This kind of enthusiasm and attention go to prove that, as Kevin said, "the coffee roaster is the living, beating heart of Starbucks."

When Dave is asked which coffee makes its way into his briefcase at the end of the day, he answers: "In that respect, I am like a sultan with a couple dozen mistresses. There are fifteen or more coffees I could grow old and die with, but I'm glad I don't have to choose just one of them. For me it's very seasonal. In summer it's the Ethiopian Sidamos, in spring the new crop of Central Americans; in fall the Kenya coffee seems to have a lot of heft, snap and crackle; and in the winter I drink the Indonesians for their depth, earthiness, and warmth."

KALADI BROTHERS
Anchorage, Alaska

What do two Seattle men in their mid-twenties do if they want to make a million dollars? They buy an espresso machine of course, move to Anchorage, and sell cappuccino to tourists in the streets. That's what Mark Overly and

Brad Bigelow did anyway, and although they're not yet millionaires, they do have a flourishing coffee business. Kaladi Bros. takes its name from the famous myth of the goatherd Kaladi, who, as the story goes, discovered coffee one day when he wondered what was making his goats so frisky. As it turned out, they were eating coffee cherries. The focus of Kaladi Bros. coffee is not goatherding but rather, according to Mark, supplying the restaurant trade with high-quality coffee. "When you go to a restaurant the meal is great up until the point they bring the coffee. The last two years we have moved into the direction of improving cup quality in food service." Kaladi Bros. also has accounts selling whole beans in liquor stores, and operates a retail account with a grocery chain throughout the bush communities of Alaska. Coffee is flown into small Eskimo villages, where by Mark's accounting, there is a higher percentage of whole-bean coffee drinkers than in the city.

The roasting at Kaladi is done with a fresh-air roaster as opposed to a drum or barrel roaster. Air is forced up into a combustion chamber off to the side, while the coffee beans sit on a grated bed. This means the coffee is never scorched or in contact with hot metal. Their other secret of success is freezing the coffee almost immediately after roasting. "There is a greater intensity of flavor preserved by freezing the coffee immediately. Coffee derives its flavor from gases. The only way to keep these gases from escaping is to freeze. We suggest to our customers that they leave the beans frozen and only take out what they need."

Kaladi is staying out of the retail market for now, because, as Mark says, "Until the consumer can understand going to the frozen section to buy coffee, we're not the right company for retail." Although consumers may still find it strange to buy coffee from the freezer, Mark feels there is definitely an increased awareness. "Customers have a taste for coffee, and they are demanding quality." The most frustrating area for Mark, as it is for many coffee retailers, is that of decaffeinated coffee. "This is an age of stress, and there are many businesses who capitalize on people's paranoia. We use direct-process decaf for the restaurant trade because it tastes significantly better." The concern at Kaladi Bros. is first and foremost quality. They do carry Swiss water process for customers who request it. "Our policy is open door. We try to get out as much information as possible about our products." This open-door policy goes hand in hand with what Mark feels is the purpose of the gourmet trade: "to make quality coffee more accessible to everyone."

CAFE DEL MUNDO
Anchorage, Alaska

In January 1973, after graduating from Sonoma State College in Northern California, Perry Merkel spent a holiday driving through Mexico, Guatemala, and El Salvador. After a visit to Antigua, Guatemala, he decided to bring back some coffee. Loaded with ten kilos of green Antigua coffee, Perry arrived in San Francisco and began searching for someone to roast the beans for him. After being turned down by every roaster he approached, he purchased a stovetop roaster, and thus began his coffee career.

In 1974, Perry moved to Anchorage, Alaska. He quickly discovered that there were no roasting operations in the state. After eight months of trying to convince his mother that coffee roasting was more than a passing whim, she loaned him his first capital. Cafe del Mundo was born, and specialty-coffee roasting was introduced to Alaska.

The initial operations were limited to supplying a few wholesale accounts. Roasting was done in a small ten-pound roaster in a converted greenhouse. This quickly became inadequate. Perry invested in a thirty-pound roaster and opened a small retail shop in 1979.

The demand for fresh-roasted coffees, both wholesale and retail, increased substantially. In 1982 Perry moved his roaster to a larger and better midtown retail location. The new shop provides lots of space for whole-bean coffees and tables for customers to enjoy their daily cappuccinos and local newspaper. In 1984 it became necessary to find separate quarters for the roasting and wholesale part of the business. A warehouse was bought and a ninety-kilo Probat roaster installed. In 1988 a second coffeehouse was opened in downtown Anchorage.

"The best thing about being in the specialty-coffee business is the product itself," says Perry. In roasting, Perry prefers the full-city roast, a roast that ends just before the oils begin to bead on the surface of the bean. "While I can't deny the popularity of darker roasts, I personally don't prefer them." Of course there is the other extreme: "That very first roast of Guatemalans was horribly under-roasted. It made commercial roasts look good. There is nothing more atrocious than under-roasted coffee. To attain the perfect roast you have to realize that there is an art and a science involved." But the most important roasting advice from Perry is: "Whatever you're doing, be consistent."

A personal favorite over the years has been Kenyans, Kirinyaga Estate being the current offering at Cafe del Mundo. Costa Rican SHB, Guatemala Antigua, and Sumatra Mandheling also make the top of the coffee list. "People are missing out on so much," Perry believes. "They don't deviate from their favorite." Perry's attachment to coffee is well witnessed by the number of steps from his bed to the espresso machine: precious few of them. "Every morning begins with a double espresso. I don't have time to steam the milk, and so I just go for voltage."

Perry's pride in his coffees is seen by his presence in the stores. He arrives early and spends time each day, including Saturdays, waiting on customers. He enjoys chatting with the regulars and meeting the newcomers.

Coffee is a passion for Perry, one he easily shares. "Coffee is a product that people enjoy as much as they need. I feel good offering a quality product that touches people on various levels. My coffeehouses provide more for the community than just a good cup of coffee. People come to start their day, read the paper, meet friends, or sit quietly writing letters or finishing projects. On any given day you will find all types of people at my stores: business people, housewives, students, and tourists. They all find a common ground with our espresso and cappuccinos. I take a lot of pride in that."

HERITAGE COFFEE
Juneau, Alaska

Grady Saunders doesn't have a lifelong history of loving coffee. In fact, he admits that he never drank coffee until he visited Europe. "Before that I couldn't stand coffee." But then came that first cup of espresso. He immediately came back to the states and began his search for good coffee, finding it at Peet's in Berkeley. This provided a short-term solution, for when Grady moved to Alaska he found that there wasn't anything comparable in the area. "Friends would buy coffee in the Bay Area and mail it to me. Soon friends in Alaska began to say 'order some for me.' Before I knew it, I was having twenty pounds shipped up here." This growing interest in good coffee got Grady to thinking, and in 1974 he contacted Starbucks in Seattle, where he met Jerry Baldwin. He describes his first few weeks in business: "I bought equipment from people Jerry told me about, and opened shortly before Thanksgiving. I sold out stock on all of my coffees five times before Christmas."

Grady attributes the success of specialty coffee in Alaska to the natural inclination of Alaskans to educate themselves about what they consume. "The population in Alaska has many relocated San Francisco and New York natives. Growth in specialty coffee is due mainly to education. We felt it was more important to educate people than to make coffee cheap, and we let the product speak for itself. We strive to sell the best possible product, and to show how much heart and hard work goes into getting that simple cup of coffee. It's easy for people to take that cup for granted, but it probably passed through a couple hundred pairs of hands before it got here. And it's still inexpensive!"

His customers obviously agree, because today, along with the Heritage Coffee retail store, Grady runs a whole-sale business and full office service. "We started office service right away with the idea that if you want to have good coffee, why wait until you get home?" He also distributes throughout Alaska with a successful mail-order business, but don't look for Heritage in other states yet. "Unless you've got roasters conveniently located I don't think you can keep the quality of coffee consistent. The idea and theory behind gourmet coffee is a roaster in every neighborhood."

Perhaps one of the most interesting aspects of Heritage's coffees is that you can find them on grocery store shelves. For Grady this was one of the hardest growth decisions. "It took a long time to decide to go into grocery stores, because I thought stores wouldn't handle coffee properly. There is a large difference between coffee that is two days' roasted and what you normally get on the grocery store shelf." To avoid these problems Grady has kept total control. "We roast and deliver twice a week, and everything is dated. We pull off whatever is still on the shelf, so that nothing lasts two weeks."

The variety of coffee Heritage sells is fairly large, and includes about fifteen flavored coffees. Five to six flavors are kept in the store and rotated on a weekly basis. Grady himself doesn't drink the flavors, but this has nothing to do with their quality. He explains, "I like coffee for itself. I enjoy the flavor and subtle characteristics of the different estate coffees." Heritage also carries all types of decaf, although they've moved away from chemically decaffeinated coffee. "In Alaska when we tried to sell methylene-chloride coffee people wouldn't buy it. People here have a tendency to consume massive amounts of information through newspapers, etc. They question processes much more." For himself, Grady believes that the chemical-processed decaf holds body better and has more flavor.

The market in Alaska has seen some changes in the fifteen years Grady has been serving coffee. "Younger people are coming back to drinking coffee. People out of the teen years want something more sophisticated. I think espresso cafes have done this." And although there is concern about chemicals, the decaf market itself has doubled, and the flavored market has also enjoyed some growth. Grady observes, "The gourmet market has gotten stronger, so more coffees have become available. You can get coffees today like Mocha Mattari, although you have to wonder how all these people get this coffee when only so much is available."

Roasting is central to the success of Heritage. When discussing his own roasting technique Grady stresses intense observation. "I roast by nose and color. The color of the beans is preliminary; the smell is the final judgment. It's a tedious job, but it's really critical that roasting be considered an art. Every batch is like a painting: you have to pay attention or it becomes a scribble." To be consistent is also important. "French roast customers will scream if you get it darker one time and lighter the next. Every coffee has its optimum roast, which is dependent on a number of things: density, age of bean, what crop."

After achieving that optimum roast, what makes the optimum cup for Grady? "My favorites change all the time, but the longest-running is a good Guatemalan or Sumatra." For Grady, however, the beauty of owning a coffee business is being able to brew different varieties at home and in the store. His perfect cup consists of coffee brewed by hand. "I use the simple Melitta-style method. I also like French presses, but I like the cone better." The truth be known, now that Grady has an espresso machine, he drinks espresso almost exclusively.

After fifteen years of selling coffee, to Grady the most rewarding thing about Heritage is the people. "It's a product that customers really enjoy. They want to experiment, ask questions. Coffee brings out joy in all your customers. But people are the number-one thing about being in the specialty-coffee business." He means not just customers, but also people in the business. "For a competitive business, people are really open and willing to talk about what they do." This willingness to exchange knowledge was most recently brought home to Grady on an SCAA [Specialty Coffee Association of America] trip to Africa. "We were all sitting on a veranda talking about coffee. You wouldn't find people from Coca-Cola or Pepsi, or GM or Ford, doing the same thing."

COFFEE'S
JOURNEY
from
MOUNTAIN
to
MARKET

THE PRODUCTION OF COFFEE IS A RELATIVELY young science. Because many of the sources of coffee beans are in Third World countries, the success of coffee production has been measured by the amount of coffee grown. Concern on the part of the grower as to whether his coffee actually tastes good is a recent (and still rare) phenomenon in the history of this commodity. In most coffee-producing areas, neither the grower, the picker, nor the government extension agent is concerned about anything but yield. On a recent trip to the Kona Coast of Hawaii I was amazed at the rhapsodizing of some transplanted gentlemen farmers with regard to their farming techniques and their concern for quality. On two separate occasions I asked farmers what their coffee tasted like and both were quite surprised. One replied, "You know, I never thought about that. How would I go about knowing that?"

Varietal distinctiveness is not an industry term but a madeup phrase, at least as it appears here. Unlike wine, which really does have varietal distinctiveness, all great coffee comes from the same tree, *Coffea arabica*. What accounts for the distinguishing taste characteristics (other than the care taken in processing it, roasting it, storing it) is the soil, weather, and air in which it is grown. For example, Sumatran and Guatemalan coffees taste very different, the former being rich and full bodied, the latter clean and crisp. From a chemical standpoint, these differences can be explained by the lightest and most delicate of the flavor volatiles found in coffee. These substances are the most susceptible to the various pitfalls surrounding coffee's transportation from jungle to port town to kitchen: high storage temperatures, staling, humidity.

✄ WHERE COFFEE IS GROWN ✄

The perfect climate for coffee production exists in a rather small cross-section of the world, between the latitudes of 25° north and 25° south of the equator. (See "A Coffee-Lover's Guide to the World of Coffee," page 38, for descriptions of coffees from various coffee-growing regions.) The coffee plant is rather particular about temperature. Changes of more than 20° in a twenty-four hour period, or temperatures of over 70° (except in rare instances of high humidity) tend to have harmful effects on production. In general, coffee trees are comfortable where people are. If the climate is apt to make people bundle up or to be excessively hot, particularly during flowering and fruit development, the trees are not likely to do well. Altitude also plays an important factor. In fact, most producing countries tend to grade their coffees according to the altitude at which they were grown. Hence the abundance of advertising phrases such as "mountain grown" and "high grown." The world's best coffees are generally grown at between five and eight thousand feet. At the San Sebastian estate in

Picking Coffee

Antigua, Guatemala, there are some trial plantings at nine thousand feet, but preliminary results indicate this elevation may be too cold for the temperature-sensitive coffee trees.

HOW COFFEE IS GROWN

The coffee farm consists of a nursery and an orchard of coffee trees. That's it. As simple as any vineyard—which, as any viticulturist will tell you, is very complicated. For starters, the types of trees that are available to the sophisticated coffee farmer are vast in number.

Considerations of quality vs. production in light of weather patterns, soil profiles, and so on, exist, but often certain trees are grown in certain regions as a matter of tradition, and to change that would mean changing the interaction between man and tree, a relationship that is often deeply ingrained. While *C. typica* needs certain treatment from seedling to its first transplantation until its final planting and subsequent pruning, *C. bourbon* requires different treatment. Unless the farmer is willing to reeducate his workers on the vagaries of the new variety he may be well advised to plant what his neighbors have been planting for the last hundred years or so. Tree types have changed over time, of course, but quality has not been the primary consideration. Hardier, higher-yielding varieties such as *cattura* have replaced bourbon and typica plantings throughout the world. Many farmers claim that the flavor is indistinguishable from that of the older varieties, given proper fertilization and irrigation. This group contends that soil and weather patterns contribute to a coffee's flavor more than does tree variety. In controlled tastings at Finca San Sebastian, for instance, coffees from two plots were compared—one *cattura* and one 80 percent *bourbon*—and there were no detectable differences. Yet whenever I have tasted coffees that instantly seem to have a special nobility and a greater complexity, they have unerringly been either bourbon or typica in origin. (One of these was from an area called Nuevo Segovia in northern Nicaragua near the Honduran border, another from the farm of Mr. Okumura on the Kona Coast of Hawaii, and another from Pampojilá, an estate in Sololá, Guatemala.)

Generally, stock for new coffee trees is grown from seeds generated from trees already growing on the farm. Caring for the coffee tree itself is critical to the nature of the final product. Seeds and seedlings must be carefully planted. After germination, the seedlings are transferred to nursery beds or plastic bags. One man usually has the responsibility of managing the nursery. A coffee tree nursery is usually a single block of land kept under some kind of mesh netting that filters out direct sunlight. Young seedlings grow slowly and require careful replanting; they are sensitive to having either too much room for their roots, or too little. A nursery manager of a farm that produces five thousand bags or more has a long day of planting, replanting, watering, fertilizing, and weeding. Coffee seedlings are very delicate, so the work requires a great deal of patience. It takes at least three years for most varieties to begin producing fruit (the older bourbon varieties often needed seven years of development). Some research has been done on the possibility of grafting arabica onto robusta root stock, but, while results were good, real-world practices don't allow for such sophisticated skills on most coffee farms, although they may be found on some large-scale farms.

The transfer from nursery to plantation is the most delicate part of the process. A seedling that is mishandled may die anywhere from two weeks to two years after it is planted, which can mean a tremendous loss of both money and effort. Soil chemistry is carefully watched in commercial operations in order to increase output. Coffee trees require certain nutrients to produce in economically viable quantities. Worldwide, N-P-K (nitrogen, phosphorus, potassium) fertilizer is the generic and preferred application. Findings indicate that a soil rich in these trace elements will yield a coffee more complex in character: nitrogen in soil gives rise to sparkling acidity in the cup; proper concentrations of potassium in the soil turns out fuller-bodied coffees; and phosphorus, while having no bearing on coffee in

(*text continues on page 166*)

Organic Coffee

The interest in organic coffee has been part of the wider trend towards healthier eating. *Organic* is a term that has evolved to refer to a product grown without the use of any chemicals including chemical fertilizer. Without fertilizer, however, coffee production is severely hindered. Particularly on older farms, production may fall off as much as 70 percent. Furthermore, without proper nutrition the final product will be a thin and lifeless brew. A coffee grown entirely without fertilizer would not only lack quality, but production would be so inefficient that it would be three to four times more expensive than even the better specialty coffees. Generally, farms not using fertilizer are those going untended or producing too little to harvest, and this usually signals a downward financial spiral from which few farmers can recover.

Chris Shepherd of Clean Foods has been selling an organic coffee called Cafe Altura since 1980, certified by Demeter. (Demeter Association of America is an independent, nonprofit foundation that visits farms to evaluate and certify implementation of organic farming practices.) His experience in organic coffee farming is extensive, and while he agrees that absence of fertilizer decreases yield, he shared with us ways in which farms combat this. Fertilizing without chemicals is done by composting. Composting is extensive on organic coffee farms, especially in the nursery. Farmers also enrich the soil's phosphate level by grinding up rocks, a natural source of the mineral, and by planting chalum shade trees, which help to fix nitrogen in the soil.

The easy question might be, "What about manure?" The trouble is that in most coffee-growing regions of the world there is very little manure to go around, primarily because the ownership of a head of cattle is something like owning a Mercedes in the United States. What manure is available is primarily applied to food crops. Additionally, the presence of manure in areas around the trees would make working around them unpleasant, as coffee trees require constant tending. While farms like those under the supervision of Chris Shepherd use composting, the use of "organic fertilizer" is (as any gardener knows) not all that simple. Composting requires a little skill and is unknown in most coffee-growing areas. I have seen farmers who used bad composting methods actually reduce their production. Also, the right organic materials for making good organic fertilizer are often not as available as they are in our garbage-rich society.

For pesticide and fungicide control, the farms Chris works with have been employing ingenious methods. Wasps are used to combat a coffee pest called *broca,* and fungus is used to combat rust, or *roya.*

Coffees that are grown by such agricultural methods are available, but their authenticity is difficult to establish. The buyer must rely on the word of the supplier that the product is free from adulterants. Because the coffee bean is an embryo protected by layers of membrane and pulp during much of its development, chemical residues are infinitesimally small compared to those in other kinds of produce. And unlike fresh vegetables and fruits, coffee is roasted at high temperatures that break down a lot of chemicals. Drinking organic coffee, then, is less a question of health concerns than one of a general policy of supporting organic agriculture.

Gary Talboy and Jeff Ferguson of Coffee Bean International in Seattle are two of the most reliable and knowledgeable suppliers of organic coffee. Their organic coffee, Cafe Tierra, is certified by the Organic Crop Improvement Association (OCIA) of North America. Gary explains some of the more important concerns they have as suppliers of certified organic coffee, and what the consumer interested in this product should look for:

"We got involved in organic coffee through the back door. Jeff got involved in organic foods, and we recognized it as a growing market. If you collect information and find out the amount of poisons we ingest everyday, you'd be concerned too. The first thing we did was look for easiest possible sources. We soon learned that the product needed to be documentable. So we did lab tests looking for residues. After attending health food shows and seminars we soon realized that didn't prove anything.

"*Residue free* and *organically grown* are two very different terms. Residue free simply means determining what level of contaminant you're going to look for, and contaminants generally appear in parts per million (ppm). There's a lot of things that can be in the product and not show up; and another thing to remember is that the plant changes chemicals through photosynthesis.

"Organically grown as opposed to residue free relates to what agricultural practices are applied, how long have they been applied, and what are the controls in place. The controls have to be monitored on an annual basis. You must go back at harvest every year and test the soil, leaf tissue, and cherry tissue, since this is where residues show up. This must be done by an outside objective source, a trained agronomist.

"As a buyer, you cannot expect Third World farmers to recognize and appreciate the critical importance of a no-compromise attitude towards organic farming. There are too many variables in their lives. Survival is the number-one concern, which places the farmers at the opposite end of organic thinking. Most important and profound, if you want organic you can't use fertilizer, so that if you really grow organic, you get low yield. This means that for most coffee farmers, the energy, education, and impetus to grow organic just isn't there. Unless, of course, you get paid a big premium to do it. If it says *organic* and it isn't more expensive, chances are that it isn't organic, although expense is certainly no guarantee of authenticity.

"The industry must keep *organic* from becoming a word that is as meaningless as *natural*. To do this we need to generate urgency about maintaining the integrity of the word as well as the product, making sure that there is documentation that meets the above standards."

the final cup, helps to develop a strong and healthy root system. Generally, the more balanced the soil, the better the coffee.

In vineyards it is often said that the finest grapes come from "stressed" vines, which are plants growing under less than optimal conditions. The organism supposedly devotes all its energies to its reproductive system with hopes of better times for the next generation. Whether or not this is true for grapes, it is undeniable that the best-tasting coffee grows in the thin air and the rocky soil of places such as the ridges of Central America and Africa.

The largest threats to coffee production in Central America are insects and fungus. In an effort to alleviate these threats farmers must purchase costly chemicals. This added expense can easily turn profit into loss for a struggling coffee farm. Some of these chemicals are currently outlawed in the United States (but still produced by American companies and sold to foreign countries). These pesticides constitute health problems not only for the farmer, but are also of concern to health-conscious consumers, although usually no chemicals can be found in the coffee. We've had coffees tested numerous times and have never found significant amounts of residue. Fortunately for the quality-conscious consumer, coffees grown at higher altitudes, which are also the best coffees, are the least susceptible to pests. The thin air does not support mold or fungus as well as do the lower altitudes.

In some areas coffee trees tend to flower throughout the year with only a brief resting period, which generally occurs during the first month of the season. In other areas the trees may flower more than once but will do so all at once, within a short period of time. The amount and pattern of rainfall has much to do with how the trees flower. (Some believe that the best coffees are those that have distinct dry periods and therefore flower only once.) The beginning of the season varies according to location, so that it's January for the northern hemisphere, June for the southern. There are no set rules in harvesting coffee. In Guatemala, coffee is picked in the fall and early winter; in Colombia, it is harvested nearly all year round. As the flowers close, the coffee cherry begins to develop. These cherries become sweet and delicate when ripe, preserving the orange and jasmine essences of the blossoms.

≫ HOW COFFEE IS PROCESSED ≪

When the fruit is ripe and glossy red, usually some six to nine months after blossoming, the cherries are harvested. (One way to distinguish ripeness is to squeeze the fruit gently between thumb and forefinger. If the cherry is ripe, the seed will be expelled easily from the fruit.) Coffee must be picked when the cherries are fully ripe, because only mature fruit will yield high-quality coffee. Time is of the essence, as the period between ripe and overripe is only a matter of days. Overripe cherries, which turn a dark red or purple, can degrade quality. If left on the tree too long the cherries may ferment, a process that affects not only the fruit but the seed, and often results in what is known in the trade as a "stinker." Other taints from overripe fruit may be caused by mold or rotting, as the surface of the fruit tends to split when overripe, becoming a haven for pests and diseases. Taints from underripe cherries are a more common problem, however.

Obtaining only ripe fruit is not an easy matter, as the harvesting process is complicated by the number of flowerings and the fact that all the different stages of maturation may be present at one time and on the same branch. At higher elevations, where better coffee is grown, ripening is particularly uneven. Because of this there are usually several picking rounds at intervals of one to two weeks.

To avoid differing harvest times, some countries have implemented chemical ripeners (such as a growth substance called ethephon), which can be used to advance ripening in hard green berries by two to four weeks, depending on the concentration sprayed. Although there is no research available on the effects of chemical ripening, it is my opinion that (as with many other modern methods of production) efforts to speed up natural processes result in a loss of coffee's distinct characteristics.

• Handle with Care •

Harvesting for a top-quality coffee also requires that the actual process of picking be done carefully. The cherries should be kept as intact as possible, and care should be taken to keep foreign matter such as stones, wood, or leaves out of the harvesting container. In countries where the "dry method" of processing (see below) is utilized, these criteria are generally not met. Instead, coffee is "milked" from the trees. Milking is stripping an entire branch of its cherries, whether ripe, unripe, infested, or empty. Twigs and stones are sorted out later. Not only does this tend to damage the foliage, but—not surprisingly—it results in a poor-quality coffee. Places such as Brazil have been searching for a mechanized way of harvesting coffee, but as yet with no success. Machines that shake the stem to release the fruit result in root damage, while machines that shake the branches result in broken or bent branches. The only option for producing high-quality coffee is hand picking.

Of course, there are risks involved in hiring a work force that is paid on the basis of pounds picked, many of which mirror those already mentioned. A good picker will take 1½ days to fill a coffee bag, a yield of approximately 150 pounds. In an emphasis on quantity above all else, little care is taken of the tree's well-being. Branches may be damaged by workers climbing to reach the uppermost cherries. Branches can also be broken or bent from being pulled down within picking reach. Some estates, such as San Sebastian, however, seem to have solved these problems (see page 177).

• *Is Your Coffee All Washed Up?* •

Once the cherries are harvested, two processes are used to separate the fruit from the seed. The first process, used for all coffees referred to as "washed," is the "wet" method. Harvested fruit is fed into machines, which by one method or another scrape the fruit from the seed. When run through water, the pulp, being lighter than the seeds, floats to the top and is pumped away. The seeds are sluiced from the bottom and fed into storage tanks, where they may sit for a day or so, depending on their size. This holdover in the water container allows the beans to ferment, which breaks down the mucillage coating that still covers the coffee beans and gives the coffee slightly more acidity. (*Acidity,* in coffee terms, unlike its common connotation, is a positive attribute. Acidity makes coffee sparkle in the cup. See page 25 for more about the quality of acidity.) The "dry" process is simply a drying of the fruit, usually on concrete patios, and a subsequent separation of the dried fruit from the seed. In the dry process, the fermentation and washing stages are omitted. This results in coffee in which the acidity becomes muted but body and mouthfeel increase. Unwashed coffees have a characteristic earthy taste, best represented by Sumatras (although Sumatran coffee may actually undergo part of the washing process).

• *From Tanning to Tumbling* •

The drying stage of coffee processing has undergone some technical changes. Originally coffee was dried on wooden boards in the sun, which limited the coffees' heat absorption from the sun and caused an unpleasant tendency to rot. Today, in most coffee-producing countries, wood has given way to concrete, which, due to greater heat absorption, can dry the beans faster. One farmer I spoke with said that with good sunlight, the drying time can be as short as ten days, while at his new mill the drying periods average five to seven days. Without good sunlight, however, the drying period can be too long for farmers who are plagued by high interest rates, increasingly overused soil, and the possibility of an unseasonable rain destroying the harvest. Drum dryers are a more efficient drying method that has recently come into practice. These giant dryers can remove moisture in a matter of hours instead of weeks. While drum dryers have obvious economic advantages, in my

Spreading Coffee in the
Sun with a Rake

opinion they also constitute another step toward reducing the distinctive varietal nuances of the world's great coffees.

• *Polishing Up the Act* •

After drying, coffee beans are still surrounded by a protective husk called the *pergamino*. At this point the beans may be stored for some time without a noticeable loss of freshness. The coffee is "milled" by being fed into machines that gently crush and rub away the pergamino. If this process is done slowly the coffee is only minimally affected. If done hurriedly it erodes the quality of the coffee. Degradation is accomplished in a simple but recurring manner: the application of too much heat too quickly. This shocks the cellular structure of the beans, causing them to give up precious flavor volatiles; it further catalyzes reactions within the bean, changing the chemical nature of flavor components; it can also cause the beans to expand and become porous, allowing oxygen to enter and the staling process to begin. A more significant loss of quality at the mill can come with exposure to cold and humidity. This pales the coffee, and in this case it may even become advantageous to heat the coffee before shipping. Many "quality" roasters have become obsessed with bean "style": the appearance of green coffee beans before they are roasted. To achieve a shiny, polished bean, producers will often over-mill their coffee. This results in a bean that is attractive in appearance but lacking any protective covering. The result, once again, is loss of flavor. If done carefully, however, polishing can aid the processor in search of higher quality, as the removal of the silverskin makes photoelectric sorting devices work with increased efficiency. The photosensitive cell can more easily identify defects in beans if they have first been polished. As in other phases of production, this step works best when done unhurriedly, much like the way we like to drink our coffee.

SORTING AND GRADING DRIED GREEN BEANS

The last step before coffee is ready to be exported is sorting. Sorting is done on the basis of the size, density, and color of the beans, although each of these criteria is not always pertinent. To roast evenly the beans all must be roughly the same size. If the coffee is from one area and has been grown at a consistent altitude and climate, the bean size and density will not vary much. While there is no agreed-upon ideal bean size, many roasters prefer larger beans, simply for the sake of the beans' appearance when roasted. Many first-quality, high-grown coffees will be well below average in size, and many big-beaned lots often end up tasting lifeless. There are always some defective beans in any given lot, either misshapen or miscolored, and these must be removed to prevent any taints entering the final cup.

Today more sorting is done by electronic weighing, sorting, and color-detection equipment than with the human eye. But, as we've stressed continually, quality coffee requires human intervention. Some degree of hand sorting must be employed, since even a few defects per pound can destroy the taste of a fine coffee.

After being carefully picked over, green coffee beans are sorted by size, density, and color, then finally rechecked through hand sorting. We will discuss, as briefly as possible, some of the electronic devices currently employed to aid in this processing.

• *The Screen Test: A Bean's Big Break* •

Grading by size is generally done with the use of screening machines. The normal green coffee bean has three dimensions: length, width, and thickness. This makes it necessary for screening devices to work with two different perforations: round holes and slot holes. Both flat and drum screen machines operate this way, by dividing the product into groups of various sizes, and sorting out coarse and fine impurities. Drum machines consist of a series of screens through which coffee is fed. The beans are kept moving with the aid of baffle plates, which rotate to clear the beans through the screens. In the first section small impurities fall through the screen, while the rest of the beans continue being fed. These beans pass through screens of different sections according to their size, so at the end you have a variety of grades and the larger impurities remain in the drum. With the flat machines, vibrating screens are located on a slight incline. Coffee moves up and down the incline with gravity, passing from one level to the next one below, the sizes being graded out as the product passes through by the larger particles being maintained on each level. Continuous cleaning of these machines is necessary to keep the perforations clear in order to get an accurate grading.

• *The Bigger You Are, the Harder You Fall* •

The density of coffee beans is measured by a device called a *catador,* or by the use of a densimetric table that is known in the trade as an "Oliver" (after a U.S. name brand). Sorting according to density, also called winnowing, is important because although the beans may be graded into groups of the same size, the groups may still contain beans of different quality. Unhulled, empty, black, or insect-infested beans may have made it through the screening process. There is disagreement as to whether density should be sorted before or after screening. General theory holds that it is best to screen first, in order to have beans of the same size but different density. In reverse order there is a risk of foreign objects of the same size making their way into the final product. The catadors discharge a strong air current below the beans while they are being fed into the machine. Heavier objects fall downwards against the current, while lighter material is carried upward. Impurities such as dust are carried out immediately with the air current, while heavier substances fall through and are sorted out by means of sieves along the shaft. Material is thus sorted out into heavy, medium, and light materials. Not only are there three weight categories, but empty and worm-eaten beans will have been sorted from the healthy beans. The Oliver, or densimetric table, has a vibrating bed with perforations that allow a strong current of air to be blown through it from below. Through the vibration of the table, the heaviest beans move toward the highest corner of the table and fall into a hopper, while the lightest objects have no contact with the table and will be carried on the air current towards the lower corner of the table and be thrown out. The separate categories between the extremes of heaviest and lightest are classified using a number of baffle plates. The beans vary in their contact with the vibrating table according to their weight and move to various levels.

• Beauty Is in the Eye of the Bean-Holder •

The coffee is now sorted according to size and specific gravity, but these categories may still contain faulty beans, which, if they are allowed to remain, will affect the final cup. Since color is almost always an indication of the beans' final flavor and fragrance, separation by color is an indispensable step for those interested in obtaining the highest-quality product. This is where the argument for human eye versus machine comes in. Because hand separation is monotonous and exhausting, as well as being a time- and cost-consuming process, many processors who sort by color rely only on machine separation. Machines that electronically measure color work by passing the bean through an optical-check cell. The beans are lit from several sides, and the light reflected by them is absorbed and measured by photoelectric cells, then compared to a given standard for brightness and color. If the bean differs from this norm, the photo-cells set off an electrical impulse that activates a short blast of air, and the rejected bean is blown out of its regular line of movement and distributed into a hopper. Good beans continue along their flight path and end up in your cup. Regardless of the impressive technology this machine utilizes, no electronic system yet developed has proved as fastidious or discerning as the trained eye. While a hand sorter can work only for relatively short periods of time, at a slower rate of approximately eighty rejected beans per minute, a human being has at her or his disposal a range of sensory perceptions and an intimate knowledge of the product that no machine can duplicate.

• *Hairy Tales of Coffee* •

Ideally, coffee should not be milled and sorted until it is about to be shipped. By storing coffee in parchment, the flavor is kept from fading, but unfortunately few exporters do this. More often than not, coffee is milled, sorted, bagged, and then stored in warm, humid coastal warehouses. This provides yet another opportunity for the coffee to undergo flavor and aroma deterioration. Coffee stored in this manner also may fall prey to mold or fungus, causing further fermentation of the beans. This fermentation attacks the fruit sugars that contribute to the coffee's body and flavor. The result is definitely a poor brew. To insure that coffee flavor is kept as intact as possible, many importers have begun writing into their contracts that the coffee is not to be milled more than ten days prior to shipment.

Biological changes to coffee beans, such as molding, often disturb many commercial roasters, but unfortunately, not always for the right reason. One roaster, having received some rather hirsute coffee, called his broker and complained. The broker noted that he had warned the roaster that this coffee might be a tad hairy and expressed regret that he was stuck with unusable coffee. To which the roaster replied, "Oh, I can blend it in, that's no problem. It's just the weight loss from all this mold that bothers me." (Since mold has a higher percentage of water than coffee, once it's burned off more weight is lost.)

PREMIUM COFFEE ESTATES

In any discussion of farming and processing there are a few shining examples. Although far from an extensive sampling of the best plantations, the following profiles will give you an idea of the kind of commitment and ideology that exist in places where farming and processing coffee goes beyond mere profit.

LA MINITA TARRAZU
Costa Rica

Located south of San Jose, in the high, rugged central mountains of Costa Rica, La Minita Plantation has over five hundred acres of coffee in production. The philosophy guiding this plantation's method of production and processing is simple: "Along with nature's basic gift of the land, growing and processing great coffee is an art. We believe that, while modern technology has its place, the skill of the artisan defines the ultimate quality of our coffee. This includes the human touch of the skilled horticulturist, a tradition of apprenticeship at the critical positions in the mill, and generations of experience handed down from father to son."

Although the farm produces and mills over one million pounds of processed green coffee every year, the plantation's flagship coffee, La Minita Tarrazu, has a very limited production of only six hundred bags (ninety thousand pounds) of coffee. An amazing amount of time and effort is invested in this coffee. It is arguably the most carefully prepared coffee in the world.

La Minita's administration views its operations as a delicate balance between economics and the people, plants, and animals that live on the plantation's land.

The soil is kept nourished, no herbicides are used, a wildlife reserve of over two hundred acres of tropical forest has been preserved, an "at cost" commissary helps to augment the staff's wages, and the plantation's health plan for serious illness covers all workers and their immediate families.

Clearly this all entails added expenses, which some producers would call luxuries, but La Minita feels that the exercise of a social and environmental conscience is an investment in the future.

SAN SEBASTIAN
Sacatepequez, Guatemala

Mario Falla grows flowers and farms coffee. The history of his family's coffee business goes back to letters written from his great-grandfather to his father dated 1903, with instructions to prepare fifty pounds of the best San Sebastian coffee for shipment to the World Fair in Orlando, Florida. The farm on which he lives in Sacatepequez, Guatemala, is still the source of this coffee, and, according to many coffee roasters and certainly according to its price, it is the best his country produces.

In Mario's opinion, the location and ecology of the area work to produce great coffee. The trees are located on approximately twelve hundred acres along the side of a mountain range. Thus the coffee plants get sun in the morning when there is still a lot of humidity due to morning dew. But attention goes beyond agricultural details. The growing and processing on the San Sebastian estate are done almost completely by hand. The exception to this rule is that they sometimes fertilize using a small tractor.

Mario took over the job from his uncle Arturo, in the same way as the position had been handed down since 1890. In the twelve years that he has been managing the farm big changes have occurred as the result of modern technological advances. Modern bathroom facilities, refrigerators, and electrical appliances have been introduced into the culture. In many cases they make their way into the homes of the finca as holiday gifts from the Falla family. "The quality of life improves on the farm through a process of teaching, not just simply giving workers an increased wage," explained Mario. "You cannot force these people to make the transition into 'modern' life. You can simply introduce new options, and then let them decide when and how they want to utilize them."

FAZENDA VISTA ALEGRE
Minas Gerais, Brazil

Two hundred years ago, Thomas Jefferson visited France and discovered a new wine that he felt was the best he had ever tasted. This wine came from an area called Sauterne, and owed its remarkable flavor to the fact that the grapes had rotted on the vine during the late summer and early fall. This rot was caused by a particular fungus called *Botrytis cinerea,* which caused the grapes to dry on the vine, concentrating the natural flavor and acquiring a particularly earthy taste from the fungus.

If Thomas Jefferson were alive today he would be raving about a unique coffee produced by Fazenda Vista Alegre in a new coffee-growing region of Southern Brazil, the 'Dry Cerrado' of Minas Gerais. Not only is FVA's Natural Dry coffee different from any other Brazilian coffee, it is different from any other coffee in the world.

The estate is owned by Eduardo Andrade, whose family has been producing coffee for more than a century. According to Sr. Andrade, until now all the coffee grown in the world was processed in one of two ways. If the growing area has enough cheap water, the coffee is washed, if not, it is dry processed. At Fazenda Vista Alegre, however, they employ an entirely new method. The coffee trees are nourished by water even after the coffee cherries achieve ripeness. Eventually, the fruit begins to darken and dry. But due to the additional nourishment the trees receive, the cherries do not fall off the tree. Instead, the beans inside the cherries continue to mature and develop a fruitiness and complexity that until now was unknown in coffee.

Natural Dry is not inexpensive. The growing period is twice that of average coffees, and it requires technology that most farms cannot afford. Compared to many other premium priced coffees however, Natural Dry is well worth the money. It is full bodied with a rich aroma reminiscent of black cherries and tobacco. Roasted lightly, the coffee retains its fruitiness and has a zesty, lemon-like aftertaste. With a darker roast, the coffee takes on an almost syrupy body with a hint of chocolatey sweetness. At any roast, the coffee has a depth of complexity that reads like a novel: cup after cup it reveals new tastes and aromas. Most notable about this coffee is its long 'finish', or aftertaste. Well after the last sip, FVA Natural Dry lingers on the palate with the sweetness and finesse of an ancient cognac.

THE BUSINESS OF COFFEE

The business of coffee, ie., exporting and importing, is, some might argue, not my field of expertise. But that, after all, is why people write books. If you're a little unclear about something, you read a book about it; if you're really confused you write a book about it. Here's my attempt at coming to grips with the muddle.

• *Exporters* •

Coffee exporting is a thankless task. Farmers see exporters as unnecessary middlemen who, because they often have large lines of credit available to them, are able to take advantage of swings in the market, buying from the farmers at the bottom of those swings and selling at the top. Even in a steady market, however, many coffee farmers see the exporter as unnecessary and parasitic: why shouldn't the farmer be able to sell direct?

The role of the coffee exporter in most producing countries is actually a fairly complicated one. Exporters simultaneously serve as marketers, financiers, and risk managers for their country's coffee production. Often, for instance, importers will contact exporters and ask for commitments on future deliveries of coffee before the beans in question have even been grown. It is up to the exporter to decide what the likely price will be for a given grade of coffee during the period for which it is requested. The exporter may simply sell the coffee to the importer "short" and figure that when the time comes he will be able to buy the coffee at a reasonable price. Alternatively, the exporter may seek a commitment from a farmer to supply a portion of his crop against the requested shipment. For such advance promises many farmers will seek advance payment: funds that can be used to buy fertilizer, pay laborers, and so on. These advance payment arrangements are often called "prefinancing."

Farmers frequently sell future commitments of coffee to exporters even when the exporters don't have an immediate market for the coffee. This usually happens when the farmer needs prefinancing or believes that the market requires him to sell at current levels. Farmers who produce particularly good or rare coffee can extract much better terms from exporters than those who do not. Many times exclusive relationships will develop between farmers and exporters that are based entirely on prefinancing agreements.

Exporters often feel that they have to buy coffee when the farmer wants to sell for fear that there will be no coffee available later when market conditions might appear more favorable. The exporters will then buy the coffee they feel they can sell but "hedge" it, that is, sell contracts deliverable to the coffee exchange in New York, thereby protecting their margin should the market go down. When they sell the actual coffee they bought from the farmer they simultaneously buy contracts from the exchange in New York to cover their earlier sales. Whatever they made or lost on the market fluctuations will be self-cancelling, and what is left is whatever they managed to make on the actual sale of the coffee.

The problem with having farmer-exporter relationships develop out of prefinancing arrangements is that such ties do not take into consideration the marketing requirements a given farmer might have. It is one of many examples of how the current system for delivering coffee to the consumer tends to see all coffees as a commodity rather than

The Short Course: Coffee Business Terminology Made Simple

Long If you're in the coffee business and you own coffee but have no customer who has agreed to buy that coffee at a fixed price, you are long. If you own a lot of coffee that is unsold and the market collapses you are long and wrong. If you own a lot of coffee and the market skyrockets, you are exceedingly smart (but you are also hated by your peers, and filled with self-loathing, knowing in your heart that you were just lucky this time).

Short If you are in the coffee business and you sell coffee that you do not have you are short. People in the coffee business "go short" when they have customers who want coffee but can find no sellers. When dealers or exporters sell coffee that they have not yet purchased, they are "making a market" for that coffee. If dealers or exporters sell coffee that they do not own and the market plummets they are smart; if it skyrockets, they are stupid.

Replacement Cost When you own coffee in the coffee business you try to sell it at replacement cost: the price you would have to pay for coffee if you were to go into the market at the time you are selling the coffee and try to buy the same kind of coffee. People in the business of roasting coffee like to refer to "replacement cost" when they are buying from dealers after the market has plummeted. Likewise, roasters view dealers who sell on the basis of replacement cost when the market skyrockets as conniving scoundrels (see corresponding definition).

Hedging If you are short or long and you can resist the temptation to try to make back all the money you lost the last time, you can "hedge your position" by buying or selling a contract on the New York or London coffee exchange. Contracts, unlike physical coffee in inventory, are fairly liquid and may be bought or sold on any business day. Therefore, if you sell coffee that you do not own you can buy a contract for the same amount of coffee from the coffee exchange. That way, if coffee prices go up and you have to buy the coffee to cover the sale you made at a higher price than you planned, then you can also sell the contract back to the exchange and break even on the market change while still preserving the margin of the original sale.

Conniving Scoundrel   Anyone who is making more money than you are in the coffee business.

International Coffee Organization   Referred to here as the ICO, the International Coffee Organization was formed primarily to bring producing and consuming nations together in an effort to stabilize prices. The International Coffee Agreement (ICA) was entered into by the ICO members in 1962 and remained in effect through most of the next three decades. With the demise of the ICA in 1989 the fate of the organization is in doubt. Most people involved both on a commercial and political level feel that the ICO will continue in some form as a forum for the expression of mutual concerns of coffee-producing and -consuming nations. The ICO also will continue to collect and publish statistical data about world coffee production. The current thinking throughout the world, for the time being at least, seems to be that any regulation of the coffee trade should be left to the rules of supply and demand.

the unique products of different farms. Certainly much of the world's coffee should be seen as nothing more than a generic product, but specialty coffee is truly the exception to the rule.

Coffees of better quality are often sold to one exporter or another out of loyalty or out of business and/or family relationships that may exist between the farmer and the exporter. Only recently have farmers started to sell to exporters with a view toward developing and improving the market for their coffee.

In some countries the farmers may export directly to importers in other countries. This is often the case when the farms have been established for two or three generations and the farmers are descendants of immigrants from the countries that the farm sells to. For example, many farms in Latin America owned by descendants of Germans who immigrated during the last century sell much of their coffee to Germany. Similarly, many Dutch-owned farms in Indonesia continue to ship to Holland as they have for over 150 years.

Farms owned by people native to coffee-producing countries often do not have the same advantageous contacts for marketing their coffees that many immigrant farmers do. Immigrants from Europe without farms of their own often found that they could get into the coffee business by buying the crops of the native growers and marketing this coffee to Europe. This is why a good percentage of the coffee-exporting companies around the world are in the hands of European immigrants. Farmers trust the exporter because he is in the country of origin (and thus they can watch him); importers feel more comfortable buying from someone who knows their language and their customs. When committing the hundreds of thousands of dollars that coffee deals involve, any added degree of trust can only help.

The exporter "system" throughout much of the coffee-producing world is populated primarily by Europeans who have been in the coffee business all their lives. Gradually, more exporting firms are coming into existence that are owned by people native to the producing country. Exporters also are becoming more conscious of marketing questions and increasing the margin they make on their coffees as opposed to the average margin paid for a particular quality of coffee. For some time Colombia has been promoting their coffee as superior to others and, in fact, they succeeded in negotiating for a specific category that only one other country was granted (Kenya) when the International Coffee Organization classifications were drawn up. From the 1960s onward, Colombia has been engaged in an active campaign to promote all Colombian coffees. Kenya also has engaged in some promotion, in addition to investing heavily in a coffee-production infrastructure that would allow for the consistent production of top-quality coffee.

For the most part, other producing countries have not had the budget and/or the motivation to engage in active promotion campaigns under the terms of the ICA. Since the economic sanctions of the ICA were suspended, however, the coffee boards of many producing countries, not to mention individual growers, have begun to consider how they might benefit from an active promotional campaign.

Guatemala, in particular, recently undertook a marketing campaign focused on the U.S. specialty trade. The campaign began with the plan of promoting five specific regional coffees: Antiguas, Atitlans, Cobans, Huehuetenangos, and Freihanes. The basic premise of regional differences in a single country is not new, but the idea of basing a promotional effort on that concept is unprecedented.

As of this writing, other countries including Costa Rica and Papua New Guinea are considering campaigns of one sort or another. The stakes are high: the world market is saturated with coffee and it is therefore of little benefit for a country to produce more coffee unless they can gain a greater share of an extremely competitive market. Therefore it is to a country's benefit to increase the margin they can make on each pound of coffee that they already produce. As part of the Guatemalan program, for instance, ANACAFE, the national association of farmers, is trying to increase production at better-quality high-grown-coffee farms while simultaneously entreating the farmers of lower-grown coffees to grow other crops. The goal is to increase the yield per acre and the percentage of profit per pound and then, and only then, to increase production in hopes of gaining a greater share of the market.

• *The Importer* •

As used in this book, the definition of the term *coffee importer* is a little different than the traditional understanding of this occupation.

In the past, a coffee importer was primarily concerned with importing large amounts of single types of coffee and selling them to roasters in the same large amounts. The coffee was generally sold in lots of 250 bags of roughly 130 to 155 pounds each. Breaking these lots up into smaller amounts was considered inconvenient. Most importers, after all, only make a profit of a couple of cents per pound (at most), and any special handling had to be avoided at all costs.

In the specialty-coffee business, one container of coffee (250 bags) often is divided up into many smaller lots. A small neighborhood roaster may order only one bag of each type of coffee at a time. In dealing with these roasters, the importer acts more as a distributor than as a commodity importer. It becomes the responsibility of the importer to be able to stock good qualities of these coffees on a "spot" basis; that is, the coffees are readily available in a warehouse as opposed to being scheduled for shipment or being in transit.

The term "importer" itself is often a misnomer in that many importers are not actually importing the coffee; they let larger firms do this and buy the best available lots from these concerns in order to distribute smaller amounts to the roasters who buy from them.

The term *broker* also is used for people selling green coffee in the specialty trade. This is not correct usage either, since a broker actually is someone who never owns the coffee but arranges the sale from one party to another and earns a commission from the buyer or the seller in the process (in the coffee business it is almost always the seller who pays the commission to the broker.)*

As a specialty importer myself I find that no one particular definition applies to the business I'm in. My company buys coffee from farmers, exporters, large coffee-trading houses, our competitors, and even back from our customers. We've sold coffee to all of the preceding, too (yes, even to farmers who've oversold their crop and need to buy part of it back).

Mostly, though, we sell to specialty roasters, who in turn sell the coffee either in shops they own or to retail operations that are owned separately; a good amount of the coffee ends up in bins in grocery stores. A lot of what we do consists of buying and importing a number of different lots of the same coffee and then matching those with the particular customers who are looking for a certain style of coffee. This means we spend a lot of time cupping coffee ourselves and discussing the coffee with our customers. I

*A term often used to describe the sellers of green coffee is *greenies*.

like to think that we're particularly committed to getting our customers exactly the right coffee, but I know that our competitors spend a lot of time doing the same thing.

As a "specialty-coffee importer," what I'm selling is a set of raw *potential* flavors, tastes, and aromas that my customers then roast into a style to their liking. So although I'm not a roaster, I have to know something about how coffees roast and what certain coffees will do when roasted in the style of a particular customer.

We keep a good deal of coffee in warehouses so that when our customers need a particular coffee, we can deliver it, whether it's Sumatra Mandheling, Kenya AA+, or Guatemala Antigua. I often think that we're more like a food-service distributor than anything else.

• *Beyond the Perfect Cup* •

Although this book is ostensibly (pervasively, thoroughly, obsessively) about coffee, it is based on the idea that people can improve the quality of their lives—and not simply those Americans who decide they'd prefer Brazil Santos #2 in the morning with their eggs, but for those Brazilians who decide it might be nice to have an egg, just one, anytime they can get one. This may be a large assumption on the part of a coffee broker whose yearly sales are often outstripped by other brokers during a good morning of trading. While claiming at least some right to wear the mantle of coffee broker, the author has no title to assume in the realm of economics. But it doesn't take a Galbraith or a Friedman to see that cash moves a bag of coffee from point A to point B. Nor does it take a Mother Teresa to see how little money it takes to keep sustenance from grinding down into misery.

There is an important and often forgotten link between the decisions we make as consumers and the options available to producers. When we consume we give livelihood to others, and what we get should not be more than we give. Terms such as *quality* and *the best* can remind us of the importance of a job well done. By buying the "best" of a given product, we also give people the opportunity to take pride in their work and to be paid a premium for it.

A pound of coffee will produce, even when brewed slightly weaker than a good Texas chili, approximately forty cups. This means that even if the average specialty coffee were to cost twenty dollars a pound, each cup would relieve us only of about fifty cents. A higher-priced pound of coffee might remind consumers that specialty coffee is not mined, like salt, but grown and processed by individuals who apply a great deal of knowledge and craft (if not art) to their professions.

It is easy to blame the coffee industry for the amount of bad coffee drunk throughout the world today. In an effort to earn higher profits and maintain their competitive edge, many roasters throughout the world resort to cheaper and cheaper coffees, which produce fouler-and-fouler tasting stuff. Many in the coffee industry respond that they are only providing consumers with what they want. But as more and more coffee drinkers come into the world, their standards for coffee drop lower and lower.

Now the coffee industry has painted itself into a corner. Many consumers have gotten used to bad coffee and don't like good coffee when they taste it. Further, they expect coffee to be very inexpensive. They associate bad coffee flavor with all the advertising on television and in print that repeatedly links bad coffee flavor to a good coffee experience (such as the après ski get-together, the intimate chat, the morning paper). Despite all this, however, some consumers want a better grade of coffee, while finding that specialty coffees taste "too strong" or "too bitter." The bitter irony for the coffee industry is that it has so thoroughly taught the consumer to drink bad coffee that they are unable to upgrade their product because it would taste too foreign to their customers.

Even among these roasters there is no denying that their coffee isn't awful. I have met many a roaster and blender who wishes he could go back to better coffee while knowing that it would price him out of the market and alienate most of his customers. Bad coffee and good coffee are easy to tell apart. The industry knows the difference, this writer knows the difference, and most consumers will know the difference if they take the time and energy to learn about coffee and to educate their palate. We can explore what makes good coffee good and we can allow for individual tastes, but we cannot argue that "it's all subjective." That's like trying to say that T.S. Eliot and Rod McKuen were both great poets.

⚜ COFFEE AS COMMODITY ⚜

The trading of grains and oil are best understood in light of the human needs that drive them. Yet the vast agricultural industry and financial network that supports the trade of coffee cannot be so explained. The intrinsic role coffee plays is fueled by a different force: desire.

The earth's support of its five and a half billion human inhabitants would cease without the production of oil and grain. Yet coffee, completely nonnutritive to man or machine, eclipses even grain in terms of international trade. The role coffee has come to play over the years has made it nearly as important as the necessities of life.

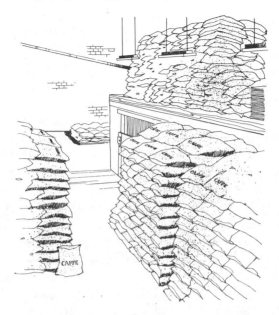

The production and sale of coffee makes the difference between economic life and death for most of the sixty nations producing it. Its production not only employs people domestically, but its export allows many countries to earn the foreign exchange necessary to remain financially viable.

The role of coffee in consuming countries is less clear. Coffee has been praised as an aid to prayer and impugned as a potion of the devil. The British blamed coffee for inciting the American Revolution. German sociologists praised it as the life blood of the Industrial Revolution. Physicians both spurn it and embrace it: it has been credited with causing heart disease, strokes, and lung cancer, and with preventing the same, with each new clinical study followed in a matter of months by a newer, opposing study.

While there are plentiful sources of information to answer the whens, wheres, whos, and hows of coffee, most of the whys are as yet unanswered. In addition, the role of coffee in producing countries has been little studied vis-a-vis changing world patterns of trade and consumption (such as how health concerns about coffee will affect the economies of producing countries, for instance).

The production of coffee has been dealt with as a problem of commodity markets, economics, and agricultural polity; coffee is usually not thought of as a product that is consumed simply because *people like the stuff*. As such, the demand for coffee from any one part of the world is extremely tenuous, and producers are at the mercy of changing patterns of consumer preference—and those tastes are changing. As the Third World becomes more industrialized, the role of coffee may diminish. But for the time being it is an essential prop in maintaining what is often only an illusion of world economic order. If the coffee drinkers of the industrialized free world stopped drinking coffee, the main result for them would be some "cold turkey" discomfort. The economic ramifications for the planet would be more extreme, and it is important to all of us that people like to drink coffee.

SECOND CUP
COFFEE CO.

Toronto, Canada

IN TORONTO, THE BREGMAN NAME IS SYN-
onymous with quality baked goods, and in
recent years, with specialty coffee. CEO and Chairman of
Second Cup Coffee Co. Michael Bregman grew up in the
food industry as the son of a successful baker. As a result of
his environment, Michael inherited a strong sense of food
retailing as well as a passion for producing the best product
possible.

While developing a strategy to expand mmmuffins Ltd.
(consisting of two other specialty bakery chains, mmmarvelous
mmmuffins and Michel's Baguette French Bakery Cafe) owners Alton McEwen and the Bregman family became interested
in the growth potential of the specialty coffee industry. In
1988 they purchased The Second Cup, a company founded in
1972 by Tom Culligan and Frank O'Dea. The Toronto based
Second Cup has since grown from 130 to 183 stores. Michael
was certain that franchising would enable the company to
grow: today 97% of its stores are franchised. In Michael's

opinion, the stores thrive because of knowledgeable, inspired and caring owner operators.

You can find a Second Cup Coffee Co. store at most malls and street corners across Canada. The philosophy that led to Second Cup's success stresses **the highest quality bean selection, excellent customer service and coffee knowledge, a carefully controlled roasting and coffee distribution system, and a single minded obsession with freshness.**

COFFEE BUYING

The Second Cup commitment to quality begins with sourcing the very best coffee beans from around the world. In fact, Second Cup buyers regularly pay a premium price to obtain the very finest coffees.

At times, Second Cup will arrange to buy all or part of a crop from a single estate. In many cases, they have coffees on an exclusive basis in Canada. One example is La Minita from Costa Rica. President Alton McEwen has found that the care and pride certain growers take in growing coffee the 'old fashioned way' can be tasted in their product. He offers customers the opportunity to experiment with unique coffees by searching out varieties that are superior to better known mass marketed coffees.

Second Cup coffee experts sample each batch they purchase, as every harvest is different and unpredictable. They search for estates that offer consistently superior coffee year after year, and discontinue selling a coffee if the crop falls below their standards. Yemen and Java are two growing regions that have produced excellent and rare coffees but, because of their inconsistent quality, Second Cup rarely purchases their crops. Instead they offer estate coffees such as La Minita which offer consistency as well as quality.

ROASTING

Even the best coffee beans can be ruined by incorrect or uneven roasting. Coffee is similar to wine; the final product is highly dependent on the handling of the raw material. Second Cup has established a unique dedicated roasting system which roasts beans in small (100-200 kg) batches, giving each coffee the individual tempering and care it needs. This stage is referred to as 'the moment of truth', and it's a step they take very seriously at Second Cup.

Second Cup believes that every bean has an ideal roast. This ideal roast is particularly important when blending coffees, as some beans should be roasted separately before being blended, while others may be roasted together. It takes a lot of patience and expertise for this process, but every Second Cup batch is screened and cupped by experts to check for consistency, flavor and appearance. According to Second Cup's strict quality control system, beans are roasted in small batches so that any problem or inconsistency can be corrected immediately.

Second Cup's own roasting philosophy is that most beans develop their fullest flavor under medium roast, retaining some of the wonderful acidity naturally present in coffee beans. Coffees such as Kenya AA and espresso blends develop well under a dark roast, while many others are at their peak under a lighter and more delicate roast...it's all a matter of taste. At Second Cup, there are five different degrees of roast, each corresponding to a number 1 through 5. The longer the roast, the darker the bean, the more assertive the flavor, and the higher the number. Their lightest roast is #1, while a #5 is the darkest. Each coffee is identified by its roast degree to assist customers in selecting the right coffee for their palate.

Second Cup recommends the following: #1 coffees as delicate tasting and excellent for breakfast or for blending with darker, heavier bodies coffees, a #3 coffee, such as the signature Royal Blend, as a perfect all day blend, and if you are looking for a bolder and more aggressive tasting coffee, the #5 roasts are full bodied and extremely flavorful with a rich after-taste.

⋙ PROPRIETARY BLENDS ⋙

Second Cup's unique signature blends are formulated using the finest coffees. Coffee experts create blends from distinctive coffees according to the motto: the sum of the parts can be greater than the whole. Royal Blend, Merchant's Blend, Espresso Classico, Espresso Forte, Buyer's Blend and several seasonal blends are available only at Second Cup. Blending is done by weight at the roasting plant to maintain consistency.

⋙ FRESHNESS AND PACKAGING ⋙

One key to excellent coffee is freshness. This requirement presents a dilemma for most coffee retailers because coffee begins to stale immediately after roasting. To maintain their strict standards of freshness, Second Cup coffee is packaged in a one-way valve pack immediately after roasting, while it is still hot.

⋙ FOR DECAFFEINATED COFFEE LOVERS ⋙

Second Cup decaffeinates coffee without sacrificing flavor because they always use the finest beans. The only difference you will find between their regular and decaffeinated coffee is caffeine. They use two processes to remove caffeine from the coffee beans: The Natural Method (CO_2-Carbon Dioxide gas) and the Swiss Water Process Method. Both are completely natural without the use of chemicals or solvents.

THE FRESHEST FLAVORS AVAILABLE

Second Cup uses only fresh roasted, high quality coffee beans for flavoring. Flavorings are custom blended by experts, and the flavored coffees are tasted frequently to guarantee quality and consistency. Because they do their own blending, Second Cup is able to create unique and intense flavor combinations not offered anywhere else.

COFFEE KNOWLEDGE

Second Cup believes that their success depends on coffee knowledge, and the ability to translate this knowledge to franchisees and customers. Their motto has always been: If you aren't interested in and passionate about coffee... you probably shouldn't be in the coffee business. In Second Cup's attempt to educate Canadian coffee drinkers, they have placed enormous emphasis on coffee knowledge, every franchisee must attend and pass Coffee College before they can operate their store. A rigorous training program organized by in-house coffee experts explores the history of coffee, its development from the cherry to the cup, and how to distinguish between varieties and growing regions. One very important marketing and education tool is the monthly newsletter *The Second Scoop*, which highlights coffee features and provides articles on recent and upcoming coffee shipments. You can pick up a copy of this newsletter at any Second Cup store in Canada.

Second Cup knows that the more knowledgeable their employees and franchisees are about coffee, the more successful they will be in educating their customers, and in recommending varieties and roast degrees to satisfy every customer's needs. It is by these means that Second Cup Coffee Co. plans to keep the growing number of coffee enthusiasts returning to their stores, and with the very finest coffees costing only a few pennies more per cup than the average supermarket coffee... a cup of the best is something everyone can afford.

VI

BREAKING
NEW
GROUNDS
in the
KITCHEN

As one of the newer flavors on humankind's menu, coffee has not acquired a wide range of uses. As flavorful as it is, we do not think of coffee as a flavoring, other than for desserts.

Part of the reason for this may be the typecasting that places coffee at the end of a meal. The most that's been done is to nudge coffee one step backward into dessert.

When cooking with coffee it is best to brew it nearly to the strength of an extract so that it will not dilute the other ingredients in the recipe. Unless the coffee needs to be cool when added, it should be brewed immediately before it is used in the recipe.

The grittiness of ground coffee, by the way, may not be as much of an obstacle as you might think. There *is* a chocolate candy with a whole coffee bean inside, and people happily eat them, well, like candy. When used to dust meat or poultry before frying or baking, ground coffee can come across much the same as coarsely ground black pepper.

Coffee is delicious when framed with sweet richness in mousses, cakes, and candies. But thinking about coffee from a fresh perspective will reveal other possibilities. Coffee has a meatiness to it, and a dry fruitiness not unlike currants; darker roasted coffees have some of the same taste components that develop in grilled foods, particularly fish. There is also a spiciness to coffee, enough clove, cinnamon, pepper to suggest a powerful north Indian curry. And it can have a chocolaty quality that hints at Mexican *moles,* not to mention the capsicum-like hotness that can be found in some darker-roasted coffees.

Delving into these particular subtleties reveals the necessity of choosing a coffee carefully when cooking with it. Obviously, it must be fresh and of good quality, but which particular coffee, from which area of the world, and roasted to which degree are also factors that must be considered. A highly acidic Kenya, for example, will have a different effect on the outcome of a dish than will the smooth, woody essence of an aged Monsoon Malabar. And, just as in brewing, the more lightly roasted coffees will reveal more of the coffee cherry's original fruitiness and acidity. Darker-roasted coffees will contribute more powerful flavors.

A unique way of transmitting the flavor of coffee to a particular food is through smoke. This can be achieved with a cold or hot smoker, and also on a grill, by dumping whole beans over the coals and letting them burn down to coals themselves. This is one of the simplest and best ways to add flavor with coffee.

The following recipes, most by professional chefs, reflect the particular inclinations of their creators. All represent a successful effort to bring the delicate components that make up coffee's flavor to each of the dishes.

A note on instant coffee: Although I would never admit to instant coffee's status as a beverage, much less recommend drinking it, it does have its uses in the kitchen, just as lesser wines will sit well in sauces, or garlic powder may serve as an adequate substitute for fresh garlic in certain cases. Therefore, you will find it included in one or two recipes.

CAPPUCCINO MUFFINS

MAKES 12 LARGE MUFFINS

This coffee-inspired recipe was found when I wandered into Opera restaurant on Ocean Street in Santa Monica. The pastry chef, Jan Purdy, created this delicious muffin using ground full-city roast Colombian or Mexican coffee.

¾ cup cake flour
1¼ cups unbleached all-purpose flour
½ cup cocoa powder
¼ cup brown sugar
¼ cup sugar
1 tablespoon baking powder
1 tablespoon ground coffee
½ teaspoon salt
6 tablespoons soft butter
1 cup sour cream
1 cup half and half
2 eggs
Zest of 2 oranges, minced
¾ cup (6 oz.) finely chopped bittersweet chocolate

Preheat the oven to 350°. Sift together the dry ingredients. Mix the butter, sour cream, half and half, and eggs until smooth. Fold in the dry ingredients, zest, and chocolate until just moistened. Fill 12 buttered muffin cups and bake until the tops are firm, approximately 15 minutes.

RUSSIAN BLACK BREAD

MAKES 2 LARGE LOAVES

While leafing through *The New Complete Book of Breads* by Bernard Clayton (Simon & Schuster) I came across this recipe for a dark Russian bread using coffee. I think the addition of ground coffee would work well in many bread recipes, particularly dark breads.

> 2 packages (4 teaspoons) active dried yeast
> About 3 ½ cups bread flour or unbleached all-purpose flour
> 4 cups pumpernickel or medium rye flour
> 1 tablespoon salt
> 2 cups whole bran cereal
> 2 tablespoons crushed caraway seeds
> 1 tablespoon *each* instant coffee and onion powder
> 1 teaspoon fennel seeds, crushed
> 2½ cups water
> ¼ cup each cider vinegar and dark molasses
> 1 square (1 ounce) unsweetened chocolate
> ¼ cup shortening
> 1 teaspoon cornstarch mixed into ½ cup cold water

In a large mixer bowl mix together the yeast, 1 cup of the white flour, and 1 cup of the pumpernickel or rye flour, the salt, bran cereal, caraway, instant coffee, onion powder, and fennel. In a saucepan combine the water, vinegar, molasses, chocolate, and shortening. Place over low heat. When the liquid is warm (the chocolate and shortening need only be soft), add to the dry ingredients. Beat at medium speed with the flat beater for 2 minutes, scraping the bowl occasionally. Add 1 cup of the white and 1 cup of the rye flour. Beat for 2 minutes, or about 100 strokes with a wooden spoon. Stir in the remaining rye flour and enough of the white flour to make a soft dough. Work the flour into the dough with a wooden spoon or a dough hook, and then turn out onto a lightly floured board.

Cover the dough with the bowl and let it rest for 15 minutes. Knead by hand until the dough is smooth and elastic. If the dough is sticky, dust it and your hands with flour. Scrape away any sticky film that forms on the work surface, and dust it afresh.

Place the dough in a bowl, cover it tightly with plastic wrap, and let sit at room temperature until doubled in bulk, about 1 hour.

Punch down the dough with the fingers and turn out onto a lightly floured work surface. Cut the dough into 2 pieces and let it rest for 5 minutes. Shape each piece into a ball, flatten slightly, and place each ball in a greased 8-inch cake pan, or both on a greased baking sheet.

Cover with a towel and let rise until the loaves have doubled in bulk, about 45 minutes.

Preheat the oven to 350° (if using a convection oven, reduce heat 40°) about 20 minutes before baking. Bake the loaves for about 1 hour, or until a metal skewer inserted in the center of a loaf comes out dry and clean. When tapped on the bottom, it will sound hard and hollow.

Meanwhile, prepare the glaze. In a small saucepan, heat the cornstarch and cold water. Cook over medium heat, stirring constantly, until the mixture boils. Let boil for 1 minute, stirring all the while. When the bread is baked, remove it from the oven and brush the loaves with the cornstarch mixture. Return the loaves to the oven for about 3 minutes, or until the glaze has set.

Remove the bread from the oven, and place on metal racks to cool.

COFFEE-BARBECUE SAUCE

MAKES 8 TO 9 CUPS

Coffee is a traditional ingredient in western barbecue sauces. It adds a rich taste that is not identifiable as coffee. This thick sauce is great with grilled chicken, or pork or beef ribs.

> 1 red bell pepper, cored, seeded, and minced
> 1 medium yellow onion, peeled and minced
> 1 fresh Anaheim chili, cored, seeded, and minced
> 1 small fresh jalapeño chili, cored, seeded, and minced
> 2 tablespoons minced fresh ginger
> 1 teaspoon freshly ground black pepper
> One 10½-ounce can beef bouillon
> ½ cup balsamic vinegar
> ½ cup light molasses
> 6 ounces freshly brewed coffee, made from
>   3 tablespoons dark-roasted coffee (use a paper filter system and run it through twice)
> 2 tablespoons maple syrup or molasses, or to taste
> 2 tablespoons Dijon mustard, or more to taste
> Salt to taste

Mix the pepper, onion, chilies, ginger, and ground pepper together in a saucepan; stir in the beef bouillon. Bring to a boil, then reduce the heat and simmer for 30 minutes. Add the balsamic vinegar, molasses, and coffee, return to a boil, and let simmer until the mixture reaches a fairly thick consistency. Add the maple syrup or molasses gradually to taste. Whisk in the mustard and add salt to taste.

COFFEE BAKED BEANS

MAKES 8 GENEROUS SERVINGS

Beans with a coffee-barbecue sauce.

1 medium yellow onion, peeled and minced
1 red bell pepper, cored, seeded, and minced
2 tablespoons minced fresh ginger
1 teaspoon freshly ground black pepper
One 10½-ounce can beef bouillon
½ cup balsamic vinegar
½ cup dark molasses
6 ounces freshly brewed *strong* coffee, made from 6
  ounces dark-roasted coffee (I use a paper filter
  system and run it through twice
2 tablespoons maple syrup or molasses
2 ample tablespoons Poupon mustard
Salt to taste
6 to 8 cups drained cooked pink beans
About 4 cups beef or chicken stock or broth (do not
use additional bouillon)
6 ounces (3 or 4 slices) bacon, cooked and drained,
or 6 ounces salt pork (optional)

Mix the chopped onion, bell pepper, ginger, and ground
pepper in a saucepan with the beef bouillon. Bring to a
boil, then simmer for 30 minutes. Add the balsamic vinegar, molasses, and coffee, return to a boil, and let simmer
until the mixture reaches a fairly thick consistency. Add
the maple syrup or additional molasses to taste. Whisk in
the mustard and salt to taste.

Preheat the oven to 400°. Put the beans in a crockpot or a
bean pot and pour the sauce over. Cook or bake at 325°F

for at least 6 hours, adding stock or broth as needed. Mix in the bacon (crumbled) if you like, or lightly boil the salt pork for 5 minutes and then place it on top of the cooking beans.

COFFEE GRAVY

MAKES I SCANT CUP, OR ENOUGH FOR 2 TO 3 STEAKS

This gravy was developed at the Stop-Yer-Heart Clinic for the Nutritionally Insane to serve over their famous country-fried porterhouse steaks.*

- 4 tablespoons butter
- ¼ cup flour
- One 10½-ounce can beef bouillon or chicken broth
- ¾ cup (6 ounces) freshly brewed coffee made from 3 tablespoons dark-roasted coffee (use a paper filter system and run it through twice)**
- 1 tablespoon heavy cream
- Salt and pepper to taste

In a saucepan, melt the butter and stir in the flour; cook and stir over low heat for 2 to 3 minutes. Whisk in the bouillon and simmer, stirring continually, until fairly thick. Add ¼ cup or so of the coffee *(don't use all ¾ cup!)*.** Heat for a minute or two longer while stirring. Whisk in the cream and season to taste with salt and pepper.

---

*You know the ones: dredged in black pepper and flour, drenched in whipped egg yolks, then deep-fried to a light golden brown in pure clarified butter.

**You need to make 6 ounces because it is difficult to get the right strength and flavor if you make a smaller amount.

COFFEE-ROSEMARY GLAZE

MAKES I CUP, OR ENOUGH FOR 4 SERVINGS

This glaze can be used for almost any sautéed meat, although I like it best with darker meats and fowl: try pork chops or a duck breast. The rosemary and the coffee seem to balance each other in this recipe, although it seems unlikely at first. I like an acidic coffee with this recipe; Kenya seems to work best.

This recipe is another example of how finely ground coffee may be used like a finely ground spice—but you can also use espresso or very strongly brewed coffee.

Meat for sautéing
Clarified butter for sautéing
2 teaspoons cornstarch (optional; if you have a
   homemade stock with lots of gelatin this is
   unnecessary)
1¼ cups chicken or beef stock or broth
2 teaspoons chopped fresh rosemary, or 3 teaspoons
   dried rosemary
Dash of ground pepper
1½ teaspoons very freshly ground Kenyan coffee, or
   ¼ cup freshly made espresso

Using a fairly small, heavy skillet or sauté pan, sauté the meat in clarified butter in small batches, browning all pieces thoroughly. Remove the cooked pieces of meat and set them aside to stay warm. Add enough additional butter to cover the bottom of the pan. Add the cornstarch, if using, and stir it completely into the butter. Add three fourths of the stock and the rosemary and pepper and cook it down until the glaze is thick enough so that it slowly swirls as you tilt the pan (it should be a little thicker than you'll want it at the end). Add the ground coffee or espresso and adjust the thickness by adding additional chicken stock or broth. Serve either over or under the sautéed meat.

VARIATIONS: *Instead of rosemary, add minced dried apricots, a dash of sugar to taste, and some grated zest of lemon to make a glaze that also works very nicely on pork, chicken, and other fowl.*

MOLE SAUCE
WITH MEXICAN CHOCOLATE AND COFFEE

MAKES 6 CUPS

This recipe was developed by Mark Gonzales, the chef at Caffé Latte in Los Angeles, who handed me the recipe as I was doing the final edits on this book (while eating at Caffé Latte). Use this as a sauce for grilled chicken or pork, or as an enchilada sauce.

6 dried ancho chilies
4 dried New Mexico chilies, or other smooth-skinned dried red chilies
6 tomatoes, halved
1 garlic head
2 onions, roasted
½ cup peanuts or pumpkin seeds (or a combination of the two)
¼ cup whole coffee beans (preferably Mexican coffee, lightly roasted)
½ cup olive or peanut oil
½ teaspoon each ground cumin, coriander, cinnamon, nutmeg, and allspice

1 bunch fresh cilantro
½ teaspoon dried oregano
1 quart hot chicken or beef stock or broth
1 cube Mexican chocolate
Salt to taste

Preheat the oven to 325°. Spread the chilies in one layer on a baking sheet and bake in the oven for 10 minutes, being careful not to let them brown. Remove and discard the stems and seeds; crumble the chilies and set aside.

Place the tomatoes skin side up under a broiler for 10 minutes, or until the skins are blackened. Let cool, then remove the skins; set aside the tomato pulp.

Partially break up the head of garlic so that the cloves are separated, but do not peel them. Place the garlic cloves in an oiled pan, cover, set over a very low heat, and roast for 45 minutes. Let cool, peel the cloves, and set the pulp aside.

Trim off both ends of the onions, place in a small roasting pan, and bake uncovered in a 350° oven for 1 hour. Let cool, peel, chop, and set aside.

Toast the nuts and/or seeds in a preheated 325° oven for 10 minutes; set aside. In a nut grinder or a rotary coffee mill, grind the coffee, nuts, and/or seeds finely.

To a saucepan, add the oil and heat. Add the nut, coffee, and seed mixture and the spices and herbs. Sauté lightly for 5 minutes. Add the hot stock or broth, salt, and bring to a boil. Break up the Mexican chocolate and add it to the mixture. Reduce the heat to low and cook the sauce, stirring occasionally, for 45 minutes. The mixture will have a tendency to stick, so take care not to let this happen. Puree in batches in a blender or food processor, then force through a sieve. Season to taste.

COFFEE-FLAVORED BUTTER OR OIL

When sautéing meat, after removing the meat from the pan, add finely ground coffee to the remaining hot butter or oil (and any spices you wish, such as cardamom or ground juniper) and stir the coffee and spices over low heat. Replace the meat and turn it in the coffee-flavored oil. Serve with a sauce if you like, but preferably with no sauce at all: the coffee-flavored butter or oil adds a deep, rich taste to almost any meat or poultry (lighter meats benefit from the sprinkling of some freshly grated lemon zest at the time of serving).

COFFEE-FLAVORED NUTTY PILAU

MAKES 6 SERVINGS

Sunil Vora, a former chef at Gaylord India in Los Angeles, now owns two restaurants called the Clay Pit, one in Los Angeles and one in Redondo Beach. He created this variation on a classic Indian dish.

The better Indian coffees have overtones of cloves, cinnamon, and cumin, all spices that are used in the country's cooking, perhaps because the coffee is stored with spices before it leaves the country. If your local merchant has it, use aged Monsoon Malabar in this recipe, although any good Indonesian will work almost as well, if not with as much reminiscence.

¼ cup raisins
¼ cup walnut halves or broken pieces
¼ cup pecans
3 tablespoons vegetable oil, preferably peanut

One 3-inch cinnamon stick, halved
6 whole cloves
6 cardamom pods
¾ cup mixed dried fruits
1½ cups basmati rice* or long-grain white rice
1½ cups strongly brewed coffee
1½ cups hot water

Mix together the raisins, walnuts, and pecans. In a heavy, medium saucepan, heat the oil over moderately high heat. Add the cinnamon, cloves, cardamom, ½ cup of the nuts and raisins, and ½ cup of the dried fruits. Sauté until the nuts are lightly browned, about 15 seconds. Stir in the rice, coffee, and hot water.

Bring to a boil, reduce the heat to low, cover, and simmer until the liquid is absorbed and the rice is tender, 25 to 30 minutes. Garnish with the remaining ¼ cup raisin-nut mixture and the remaining dried fruits.

*Available at Indian markets, specialty food markets, and often in the specialty food section of the grocery store

---

PASTA KAHAWA

MAKES 6 SERVINGS

Hugo's in West Hollywood takes their coffee very seriously. They grind their own beans to provide customers with a great cup of coffee every time. Their best brew often finds its way into the kitchen, in dishes like the following pasta. In this recipe the sweet aftertaste of artichokes is balanced by the acrid undertones of coffee. (This recipe was developed by Tom Kaplan, now the owner of Caffé Latte, when he managed Hugo's.)

3 cups baby artichokes, quartered and trimmed, or
  two 9-ounce packages thawed frozen artichoke
  hearts
1 tablespoon fresh lemon juice or vinegar
1 cup strongly brewed coffee
1½ cups heavy cream
2 tablespoons Dijon mustard
1 tablespoon chopped fresh rosemary
Salt and freshly ground white pepper to taste
2 tablespoons olive oil
½ pound fresh shiitake mushrooms, stems removed
1½ pounds fresh fettuccine

Cook the fresh artichokes in a large pot of boiling salted water acidulated with the lemon juice or vinegar until the artichokes are just tender, 10 to 15 minutes. Scoop out the fuzzy choke from each piece.

In a large non-aluminum saucepan or a flameproof casserole, marinate the artichokes in the coffee for 10 minutes.

Stir in the cream and bring to a boil. Reduce the heat to moderately low and simmer until the liquid is reduced by almost one fourth, about 10 minutes.

Blend in the mustard and rosemary. Season with salt and white pepper to taste. Remove from the heat and cover to keep warm.

Meanwhile, in a large skillet, heat the olive oil. Add the mushrooms and sauté over moderately high heat until they are lightly browned, 3 to 5 minutes. Set aside.

In a large pot, bring at least 4 quarts of salted water to a boil. Add the fettuccine and cook for 1 to 2 minutes, or until tender. Drain well.

Bring the cream and artichoke mixture to a simmer over moderately high heat. Add the pasta and toss in the cream sauce for 30 to 60 seconds. Divide the fettuccine and artichokes among 6 dinner plates and top with the sautéed mushrooms.

COFFEE BURGERS

MAKES 4 TO 6 SERVINGS

This recipe like two others in this book, uses instant coffee. Please don't be horrified by the inclusion of it in this august opus, and please, please, don't report us to the Coffee Police.

Summer is the time for barbecues and tall glasses of iced coffee. This recipe comes from Ross D. Siragusa, Jr., of Straight Creek Farm in Ft. Payne, Alabama. Straight Creek is home to one of America's premier herds of Limosin cattle. Originally from France, this beef has much less fat than most other breeds. Cattle ranchers in the United States are breeding their own herds with Limosin to produce "healthier" beef. Use the leanest ground beef you can find, or grind your own, trimming as much fat as possible before grinding.

> 1 pound Limosin or other very lean ground beef (see above)
> ¼ cup crumbled blue cheese
> 1 heaping tablespoon instant or very finely ground coffee
> 1 heaping tablespoon powdered chili mix
> 1 teaspoon Dijon mustard
> ¼ cup chopped green onions
> 1 small jalapeño pepper, cored, seeded, and minced
> ¼ cup diced red or green bell pepper
> 1 tablespoon Worcestershire sauce

Mix all the ingredients together, form into patties, and grill to desired doneness.

GRILLED COFFEE-MARINATED LAMB CHOPS

Coffee beans are highly flammable due to the natural aromatic oils they contain. In this recipe, most of the air is closed off to the grill so that the beans smoke but don't burn. You can substitute any of your favorite barbecue meats for the lamb chops. Just keep in mind that the flavor of the smoking will be much stronger for lighter meats such as chicken and turkey.

    6 to 8 lamb chops, cut 1½ inches thick
    4 cups warm strong black coffee
    1 pound Kenyan or other acidic coffee beans

Marinate the lamb chops in the coffee for 3 hours. After 2 hours, start a fire on a covered grill with half charcoal and half mesquite. Set the grill about 1½ inches above the coals. When the coals are covered with white ashes, place the lamb on the middle of the grill. Have the lid to the grill ready and close the vents most of the way. Quickly sprinkle half of the coffee beans around the outer edge of the fire on top of the coals and cover the grill immediately.

    After 5 to 10 minutes for rare or medium-rare, turn the chops and add the remaining beans. The coffee will contribute a smooth yet very hearty smoked flavor.

COFFEE-SMOKED DRUMSTICKS

MAKES 6 APPETIZER SERVINGS

Served as an appetizer, or as a main course with arugula salad in a light vinaigrette. Duck, lamb, and sirloin can be smoked by the same technique. This recipe was inspired by Barbara Tropp, who is famous for the tea-smoked duck served at her China Moon Cafe in San Francisco.

½ cup sugar
½ cup long-grain white or basmati rice
½ cup finely ground Costa Rican or New Guinean coffee
6 chicken drumsticks

Mix the sugar, rice, and coffee and place the mixture in the bottom of a wok that has been lined with heavy aluminum foil (let extra foil protrude beyond the rim). Make sure there are no seams in the lining where the smoking mixture sits. Place a rack over the mixture, and place the drumsticks on the rack. Line the wok lid with foil, letting extra foil protrude beyond the rim, and place the lid securely on top of the wok, and carefully seal the foil lining of the top to the bottom.

Gently heat the wok until the lid is just a little too hot to touch. Let the chicken smoke for about 20 minutes, then let the wok cool for about 10 minutes before opening (when you do open it I recommend doing so outside as the smoke may be heavy). The chicken should be juicy but cooked through. If it is not, cook it in a 350° oven for a few minutes longer, or until the juices run clear when the chicken is pricked with a fork.

CARDAMOM AND COFFEE–DUSTED CHICKEN

MAKES 2 TO 4 SERVINGS

This recipe was inspired by a quail recipe created by Anne Rosenzweig of Arcadia Restaurant in New York for an article I wrote for *Food & Wine Magazine* a few years ago.

Further inspiration came from a shipment of Guatemalan Antiguas that came in a few years ago. My customer, who got a sample off the dock before I did, complained bitterly that they "smelled funny." When I tasted it it reminded me of Turkish coffee flavored with cardamom, and that, in fact, is what had happened: the coffee had been stored next to some cardamom for several months before being shipped. The ground coffee is a little strange when you first bite in, but the ephemeral, smooth not-quite-coffee flavor more than makes up for it. This treatment also works well on lean game birds, pork chops, and lamb.

8 tablespoons freshly roasted *very* finely ground
    Kenyan coffee
1 teaspoon freshly ground black pepper
½ teaspoon finely ground cardamom
1 frying chicken, cut up
Grated zest of 1 lemon

Preheat the oven to 375°. Mix the coffee, pepper, and cardamom together and dust the chicken pieces with the mixture. Let the pieces sit for at least 1 hour. Bake in a flat ceramic or glass dish until tender, about 20 to 25 minutes.

CHILI GRILLED CHICKEN
IN A SPICY BELL PEPPER–ORANGE SAUCE
WITH COFFEE

MAKES 6 TO 8 SERVINGS

Barbara Figueroa has a resumé that reads like a Who's Who of America's best kitchens. Having done stints at Le Cirque and Jam's, among others in New York, Figueroa moved to Los Angeles and plied her trade at Spago in Los

Angeles. She is currently the executive chef at the Sorrento Hotel in Seattle, Washington. The following recipe illustrates the imaginative, balanced approach that is consistently reflected in her work.

2 medium dried ancho chilies
2 medium red bell peppers
1 tablespoon olive oil
¼ cup chopped onion
1 teaspoon minced garlic
1 tablespoon curry powder
½ teaspoon fennel seeds, crushed
½ teaspoon ground cumin
1 teaspoon sweet paprika
2 tablespoons strong coffee
¼ cup duck stock or chicken stock or broth
½ cup chicken stock for thinning sauce
4 tablespoons butter
5 tablespoons fresh orange juice
2 tablespoons fresh lime juice
Two 2½-pound broiling chickens, preferably free range, boned and split
2 garlic cloves, peeled and split
10 small (1 inch) dried chilies, split and seeded
Cilantro sprigs
1 orange, cut in half, thinly sliced, and cut into half circles

Cut the ancho chilies in half lengthwise. Remove the stems and seeds. Place the chilies in a small heatproof bowl and add enough boiling water to barely cover them. Let stand, covered, 30 minutes. Drain. When cool enough to handle, remove the skins.

Place the bell peppers directly over a high gas flame or under a broiler, turning them frequently until the skin is blackened all over. Place the peppers in a paper bag and let cool for 10 minutes. Remove the stems, seeds, and skins, wiping away any blackened particles with a damp cloth.

In a small saucepan, heat the olive oil over low heat. Add the onion and garlic and cook, stirring frequently, for 5 minutes, or until tender.

Add the curry powder, fennel seeds, cumin, and paprika. Cook for 3 minutes, stirring frequently.

Add the coffee, ¼ cup duck stock or chicken stock or broth. Bring to a boil, add the chilies and bell peppers, and simmer for 30 minutes, stirring occasionally.

Puree the mixture in a blender with the butter. Add the orange juice, lime juice, and additional stock or broth to thin sauce if necessary. Set the sauce aside to keep warm.

Rub the chickens with the split garlic cloves. Stuff the split chilies under the skin of the chickens. Grill or broil until the flesh is firm, yet springy. Remove the chilies from under the skin. Arrange the chickens on serving plates, and ladle the sauce around them. Garnish with cilantro sprigs and orange slices.

CARNE DE RES CON CAFE

MAKES 8 SERVINGS

Coffee can be used in meat dishes as a tenderizer, a marinade, and a subtle flavoring agent. The following recipe from El Salvador is from Copeland Marks's book of Guatemalan and Mayan recipes, *False Tongues and Sunday Bread* (M. Evans and Co., New York). Serve this dish with rice.

    3 tablespoons corn oil
    3 pounds beef chuck, cut into 2-inch cubes
    3 cups sliced onions
    1 ½ cups sliced green bell peppers

4 garlic cloves, sliced
2 cups chopped ripe tomatoes
2 cups strong coffee
½ cup tomato catsup
6 small carrots, peeled and halved

In a sauté pan or skillet, heat the oil and brown the meat well over moderate heat. Add the onions, green peppers, garlic, and tomatoes. Mix and bring to a boil.

Add the coffee and catsup. Cover the pan and continue to cook until the meat is tender, about 1½ hours. Add the carrots for the last 20 minutes. When done, the carrots will be tender and the sauce will be reduced and thickened.

COUNTRY HAM WITH RED-EYE GRAVY

MAKES 12 SERVINGS

This recipe evolved fom the longtime friendship and mutual interest in exceptional food between Regina Mirman and Los Angeles caterer, Milton Williams. Regina says, "It's yummy."

One 12- to 14-pound aged country ham
2 quarts water
1 cup honey
1 cup prepared brown mustard
½ cup light brown sugar
2 onions, sliced
2 garlic cloves, sliced
4 cups Guatamalan or other acidic coffee, such as Kenyan
2 cups rich chicken stock or broth
2 teaspoons flour mixed with 2 teaspoons water

If the ham has aged for 6 months or less, soak it in water to cover overnight in the refrigerator. If the ham has aged for 6 to 12 months, soak it for 2 to 3 days.

Scrub the ham all over well with a stiff brush and warm water. Place the ham skin side up in a large, deep roasting pan. Add the 2 quarts water. Stir in the honey, mustard, and brown sugar.

Preheat the oven to 250°. Bake the ham, basting it periodically and occasionally turning the roasting pan for even baking, until the internal temperature reaches 160°, or about 20 minutes per pound for a total of 4 to 5 hours.

Remove the ham from the oven and transfer to a platter. Reduce the liquid in the pan, stirring it over high heat until thick, 1 or 2 minutes. Pour the liquid from the pan and set aside.

Turn the oven up to 375°. Return the ham to the pan. With a knife, lightly score the ham in a crisscross pattern. Coat the ham with the cooking-liquid paste (there may be some left over). Return the pan to the oven and bake until the paste melts and glazes the ham, about 25 to 30 minutes. Brush occasionally with any extra glaze or with the pan drippings. Remove the ham from the oven and set it aside to rest.

Add the sliced onions and garlic to the pan and return it to the oven. Let cook 10 to 15 minutes, or until the onion begins to caramelize.

Deglaze the pan with the strong coffee, scraping up any particles from the pan.

Pour the contents of the pan into a saucepan. Reduce to 1 cup and add the stock or broth. Bring to a boil and simmer, skimming the surface of any fat or foam.

Stir in the flour and water mixture to thicken. Bring to a boil, season, and strain.

To serve, cut the ham into thin slices perpendicular to the bone. Arrange the ham on a platter and serve with the red-eye gravy.

RIS DE VEAU CHA CHA CHA
(Warm Veal Sweetbreads with Pinto Beans, Cinnamon, Orange, Jalapeños, and Coffee)

MAKES 6 SERVINGS

John Sedlar, chef and partner of St. Estèphe in Manhattan Beach, opened his restaurant focusing on the basics of his training in classic French cuisine. Gradually, however, he developed a more personal style, using the ingredients found near his home town, Santa Fe, New Mexico. Over the past few years, Sedlar has become one of the leading forces in American Southwest cuisine. In this recipe, the flavor of coffee is incorporated in a simple and surprisingly delicious way. This sauce also can enhance veal scallopine.

3 quarts salted water
1 ½ pounds veal sweetbreads
Ice water
1 tablespoon diced jalapeño chilies
½ teaspoon ground cinnamon
1 cup strongly brewed coffee
3 quarts water
1 cup dried pinto beans, washed
6 ounces bacon or salt pork, cut into ¼-inch dice
1 orange
½ teaspoon salt, or to taste
½ teaspoon ground pepper, or to taste
Watercress sprigs

Place the salted water in a large pot and bring to a boil over high heat. Reduce the heat to a simmer, carefully slip in the sweetbreads, and cook for 30 minutes. When the cooking time is almost over, prepare a large bowl of ice water. Drain the sweetbreads and plunge them quickly into the ice water to stop the cooking. Carefully pull off any clear membrane and veins and cut the sweetbreads into ½-inch-thick pieces. Set aside.

In a 6-quart saucepan, bring the jalapeño, cinnamon, coffee, and water to a boil. Reduce the heat, add the beans and bacon, and let simmer uncovered for about 3 ½ hours, or until the beans are tender and the liquid has a thick consistency. Grate the zest of the orange and set aside, then peel the orange and separate it into segments. Add the orange segments to the beans.

Season the sweetbread slices with salt and pepper to taste. Steam the sweetbreads over boiling water for about 4 minutes, or until warmed through. Spoon half of the sauce onto 6 large warm plates, arrange the sweetbreads on top, and drizzle the remaining sauce over them.

Garnish with grated orange zest and sprigs of watercress.

BAKED HAM WITH COFFEE GLAZE AND TURNIPS

MAKES 12 SERVINGS

Gordon Sinclair became enamored of lighter trends in French cooking in the early seventies and introduced them to Chicagoans fifteen years ago when he opened his first restaurant, Gordon. Since then many trends have been presaged there, including "California" pizzas and an ongoing interest in American cuisine.

Horrifying as it may seem, this recipe calls for instant coffee, which works because it complements the warm and hot notes of the turnips and chilies without diluting the glaze with too much liquid. Ham is usually paired with light-bodied red wines, but this glaze begs for more: try a

California Zinfandel for the added complexity needed in this dish.

1 small (about 4 to 6 pounds) bone-in fresh ham
8 cups strong coffee
4 cups pineapple juice
1 cup dry white wine
2 Spanish onions, peeled and cut into small dice
(about 1½ cups)
1 head garlic, all cloves peeled and chopped
½ cup vegetable oil
4 small tomatoes, chopped (about 2 cups)
3 small fresh hot chilies with seeds, chopped (about
⅛ cup)
¼ cup white wine vinegar
2 teaspoons ground cumin
4 tablespoons instant espresso powder, *or*
12 tablespoons instant coffee
2 cups chicken stock or broth
1 tablespoon salt
1 tablespoon ground pepper
3 pounds turnips, with their greens
4 tablespoons butter

Trim the ham of heavy fat and skin. Mix the coffee, pineapple juice, and white wine together. Place the ham in a non-aluminum container and marinate the fresh ham for 2 days in refrigerator in the coffee mixture, turning the ham 2 to 3 times daily.

To cook, drain the ham, reserving the marinade; set the ham aside.

To make the glaze, sauté the onions and garlic in the oil until translucent. Add the tomatoes and chilies and sauté a few minutes longer. Add the vinegar, cumin, instant coffee and the chicken stock or broth and cook slowly to reduce by one half. Remove from the heat, add 1 cup of the marinade, puree in a blender or food processor until very smooth, and set aside.

Preheat the oven to 300°. Season the ham well with salt and pepper and place on a roasting rack, skin side down. Brush the glaze over the ham, lightly covering the top and sides.

Bake the ham for 2½ to 3 hours, re-glazing every 30 minutes and turning it skin side up after 1½ hours.

Trim the turnips of their greens; wash the greens and set them aside. Peel and slice the turnips into thin circles. Melt the butter in a skillet and sauté the turnip slices until lightly colored and tender. Steam the greens whole over boiling water for 2 to 3 minutes. Fan the greens out on platter and place the turnip slices on top.

CHOCOLATE ESPRESSO SOUFFLÉ

MAKES 6 SERVINGS

This recipe comes from Joan Burns, a terrific cook who seems to know every great caterer and restaurant in Los Angeles.

6 ounces bittersweet chocolate
¼ cup freshly brewed espresso
Granulated sugar
3 egg yolks
4 egg whites
2 tablespoons powdered sugar, to taste
1 cup heavy cream, whipped softly and lightly sweetened
Zest of 1 orange, cut into fine julienne

Preheat the oven to 180° to 200°. Place the chocolate and espresso in a stainless steel bowl and place it in the oven until the chocolate melts. Remove from the oven and raise the oven temperature to 400°. Generously butter 6 ramekins and sprinkle the insides with sugar. When the chocolate is melted, whisk in the egg yolks and set aside in a warm place. Whip the egg whites until frothy, add the powdered sugar, and continue to whip until stiff. Do not overbeat. Fold the egg whites into the chocolate and add the orange zest. Pour into the prepared ramekins and bake for 9 to 10 minutes. Remove from the oven and serve immediately. Serve with whipped cream.

TIRAMISU

MAKES 12 SERVINGS

The most popular coffee recipes are desserts. One of my favorites is the traditional Italian tiramisu, a combination of ladyfingers, espresso, mascarpone, and chocolate. This recipe, from Chianti Ristorante, a fantastic Italian restaurant on Melrose in Los Angeles, makes one of the best tiramisus you'll ever have.

6 egg yolks
1¼ cups sugar
1¼ cups mascarpone cheese
1¾ cups heavy cream, whipped to form soft peaks
1¾ cups cold espresso
2 tablespoons brandy
2 tablespoons grappa or brandy
48 ladyfingers
Powdered unsweetened chocolate for topping

In the bowl of an electric mixer, cream the yolks and sugar until smooth. Add the mascarpone and mix on low speed for 2 minutes. Fold in the whipped cream; set aside. In a medium bowl combine the espresso, brandy, and grappa. Dip 15 of the ladyfingers one at a time into the espresso mixture and arrange in a single layer on a 10- by 15-inch platter or a baking sheet, forming a rectangle about 7 by 13 inches. Cover with half of the mascarpone-cream mixture. Repeat the layers with 15 more ladyfingers dipped in espresso mixture, then the remaining mascarpone-cream mixture. Sift the chocolate evenly over top. Halve the 18 remaining ladyfingers and arrange them vertically around edge of cake, cut sides down. Refrigerate for at least 4 hours. Cut into squares to serve.

VALENTINO

MAKES 12 TO 14 SERVINGS

This dessert recipe is enough to satisfy the sweetest of tooths—chocolate fudge with walnuts, amaretti cookies, raspberry sauce, and whipped cream. Although the coffee is not the strongest flavor of the recipe, espresso adds its own rich note to this decadent and chocolaty creation from Ciao restaurant in San Francisco.

1½ cups unsalted butter, softened
9 hard-cooked egg yolks
12 ounces semisweet chocolate, melted and slightly cooled
¾ cup prepared fudge topping
½ cup unsweetened cocoa powder
3 tablespoons brandy

2 tablespoons amaretto liqueur
1 tablespoon vanilla
6 ounces semisweet chocolate, shaved or very finely
   chopped with chef's knife
4 ounces amaretti cookies
½ cup cooled espresso coffee

Raspberry puree:
3 packages (12 ounces each) unsweetened frozen
   raspberries, thawed
6 tablespoons sugar

Garnish:
additional amaretti cookies, crushed
fresh mint sprigs

Cream butter in large mixer bowl. Force yolks through
fine sieve into butter; beat until smooth. Add melted
chocolate, fudge topping, cocoa, brandy, liqueur, and vanilla. Beat at medium speed until light and fluffy, 8 to 10
minutes. Mix in shaved chocolate. Oil a 9 × 5 loaf pan and
line smoothly with plastic wrap. Spread one-third of the
chocolate mixture in bottom of pan. Dip half the cookies,
one at a time, into coffee and arrange evenly on chocolate
layer. Cover with half the remaining chocolate mixture;
smooth top. Repeat with remaining cookies, coffee, and
chocolate mixture. Smooth top and press down firmly to
eliminate air spaces. Cover and refrigerate several hours or
overnight.

Raspberry puree: In electric blender puree the thawed
raspberries. Force through fine sieve. Mix in 6 tablespoons
sugar, or to taste. Makes 3 cups.

To serve, spoon scant 3 tablespoons raspberry puree
onto each plate. Cut loaf into slices about ¾-inch thick
with sharp knife dipped into hot water. Place a slice on

each plate. Sprinkle with additional crushed cookies and garnish with mint sprigs, if you wish. Leftover loaf can be covered and refrigerated up to 4 days.

COFFEE ICE CREAM

MAKES 12 SERVINGS

What coffee recipe section would be complete without a coffee ice cream? Attribution is uncertain—

- 1 quart heavy cream
- 7 tablespoons finely ground Sumatra or other full-bodied coffee
- 8 egg yolks
- Kahlúa or coffee liqueur
- ½ cup sugar

In a heavy saucepan, bring the heavy cream to a simmer, add the ground coffee, cover, and turn off the heat; let sit for 18 minutes. Strain through a fine strainer and heat again to a simmer.

In a bowl combine the egg yolks, liqueur, and sugar and mix until smooth.

Ladle a small amount of the cream into the yolk mixture, stirring constantly. Continue adding cream until half of it is in the yolk mixture, then return everything to the saucepan.

Cook over medium-high heat, stirring constantly from the bottom, until the cream coats a spoon thickly.

Quickly pour the cream into a bowl and set the bowl in an ice bath. When cool, freeze in an ice cream machine according to the manufacturer's instructions.

CAFÉ WALNUT

MAKES 2 SERVINGS

This recipe was born of a mistake. While cooking a dinner one night, I needed some finely ground walnuts fast and used my rotary coffee mill. In my stupor the next morning I ground my coffee in the same grinder without removing all the walnuts. The result was an interesting flavored coffee. The cardamom is a more recent refinement. Walnuts and cardamom were used to flavor coffee centuries ago, shortly after its discovery.

1¾ to 2 cups water
4 tablespoons finely ground Costa Rican or other acidic coffee
1 tablespoon finely chopped or mashed walnuts
⅛ teaspoon ground cardamom
2 tablespoons warmed heavy cream or to taste
Sugar to taste

Bring the water to a boil. Mix the chopped walnuts, cardamom, and ground coffee together and place in a paper coffee filter. Pour the hot water over. Add cream to taste and sweeten as needed.

COGNAC AND COFFEE

MAKES 2 SERVINGS

This simple recipe yields a drink that has the body of coffee liqueur without the sweetness. If you use less coffee than is

(*text continues on page 228*)

One Hundred Other Things to Do with Coffee

1. You can drink it (hot).

2. You can drink it (cold).

3. If you drink it cold, you can make ice cubes out of it so when you make iced coffee the ice cubes won't dilute the flavor.

4. You can eat the beans, one at a time. (Some people become addicted to this practice. A few beans can give you quite a caffeine jolt. Some beans are flavored or coated to make chewing more enjoyable.)

5. You can cook with it (see recipes).

6. You can barbecue with it; that is, you can smoke things with it as opposed to using it as an actual ingredient (see recipes).

7. You can grow it as a decorative indoor plant, and in the Southwest and parts of the South (where it doesn't frost) you can grow it outdoors. But don't expect to drink much; it won't produce a significant amount of cherries. Ask your local nursery if they sell coffee trees.

8. You can use used and unused coffee grounds as a soil enhancer for ferns and other acid-loving plants. The grounds preserve moisture well and encourage acetic-forming bacteria. Because of this, blueberries and evergreens are especially fond of coffee grounds. (Be careful, though, what plants you feed with coffee. I nearly killed my *ficus* with coffee grounds, and my *camellias* didn't take kindly to the stuff either. Check with your nursery before using grounds on your

prize orchids, or any other plant, for that matter.)

9. You can use coffee grounds to keep insects, snails, and slugs away. This makes sense, as the caffeine in coffee supposedly acts as an insect repellent for the coffee tree and its cherries.

10. You can use it as a dye for fabrics.

11. You can use it to color Easter eggs, for a nice natural look.

12. You can stain a pipe with it. My grandfather had a briar pipe that he loved to smoke, but he hated the color. So he sanded it down and soaked it in strong, strong coffee for a few days and then let it dry out, baked it in a low oven, burned out the bowl with a mixture of sugar and other things, and it became his favorite pipe.

13. You can paint with it. (Watercolor with your coffee when it gets cold!)

14. The Japanese take a kind of mud bath in coffee grounds, although I've never tried this.

15. I've also heard that you can use coffee as an enema, though I've never tried that either.

16. In many countries, coffee once was used as currency. While that may not work today at Neiman Marcus, in the right circles it could be used in a game of poker.

17. You can compose a cantata about it. (Bach did.)

18. You can make a fortune selling it. (No guarantees.)

19. You can lose a fortune selling it. (I could almost guarantee this, but I won't.)

20. In Guatemala, and most likely in other countries as well, they make necklaces and bracelets from varnished roasted beans.
21. You can philosophize while drinking it. (Voltaire drank seventy cups a day.)
22. You can play jacks with the beans.
23. No time to tan? Take a coffee dip. If your significant other loves coffee, this may have some pleasant side effects.
24. After driving around with large quantities of freshly roasted coffee, I found that the smell permeated my car.
25. You can write a book about it.
26. You can come up with more things to do with it, and then write and let me know about them. If your suggestions are really good, I'll add them to future editions of this book. (Keep it clean, folks.)

Tim Castle
2210 Wilshire Blvd., Suite 634
Santa Monica, CA 90403

recommended here, it will make an inexpensive cognac a bit darker and smoother. Almost any coffee can be used, but I prefer a fully roasted (oily) Guatemalan Antigua, which has always reminded me of cognac.

1 cup boiling water
1½ heaping teaspoons freshly ground Guatemalan Antigua coffee
½ cup cognac or good brandy, warmed

Pour the boiling water through a paper coffee filter in a Melitta cone and let the water drain through completely. (This gets rid of any paper taste; otherwise the brandy will taste like paper.) Add the coffee to the warm cognac and let sit for about 5 minutes. Stir the mixture and pour it through the filter. Warm it again if necessary before serving.

VARIATIONS: *You can use any hard liquor to extract the flavor of coffee; rum works well. You can then use this liquor in a variety of mixed drinks such as coffee libre: coffee-flavored rum with Coca-Cola.*

INDEX

Index

Index